THE BEST OF
THE BEATLES

ISBN 978-0-7935-2917-9

HAL•LEONARD®
CORPORATION
7777 W. BLUEMOUND RD. P.O. BOX 13819 MILWAUKEE, WI 53213

Visit Hal Leonard Online at
www.halleonard.com

2

All You Need Is Love

Electronic Organs
Upper: Flutes (or Tibias) 16', 4'
Lower: Reed 8', Diapason 8'
Pedal: 8'
Vib./Trem.: On, Fast

Drawbar Organs
Upper: 80 0800 000
Lower: (00) 7334 010
Pedal: 05
Vib./Trem.: On, Fast

Words and Music by John Lennon
and Paul McCartney

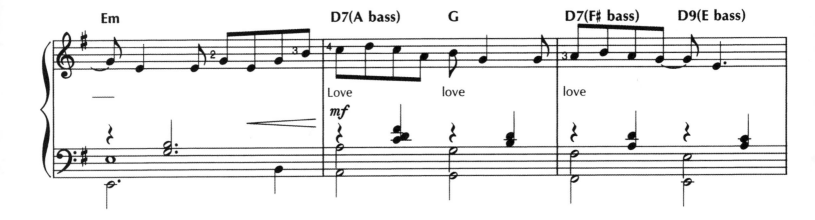

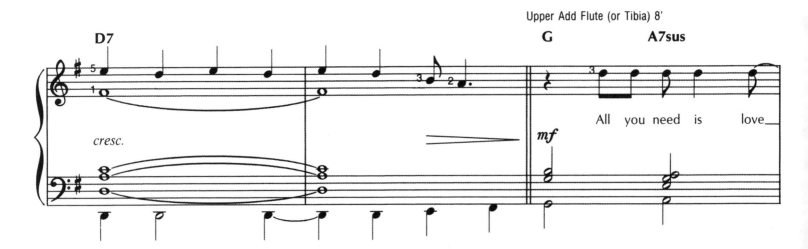

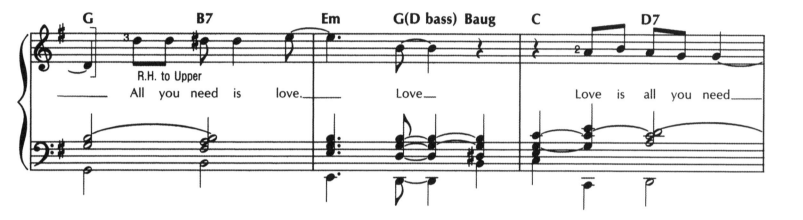

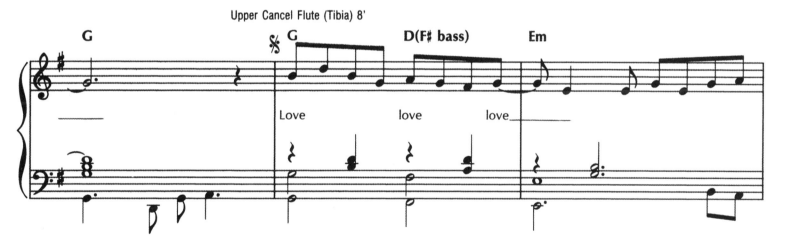

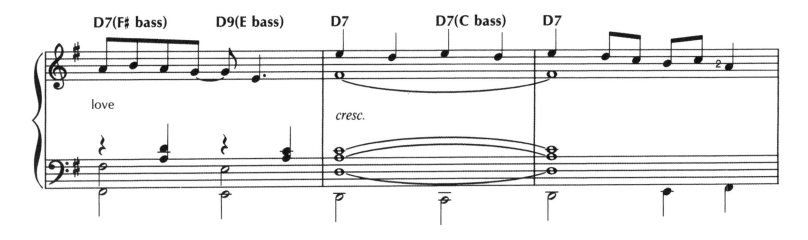

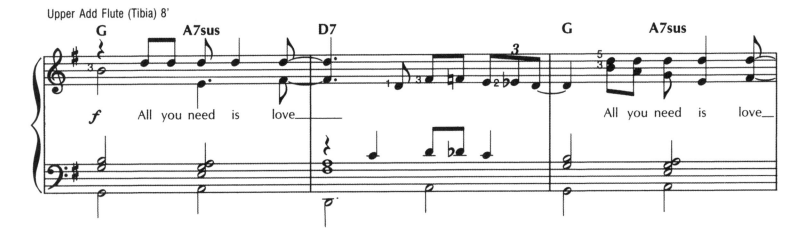

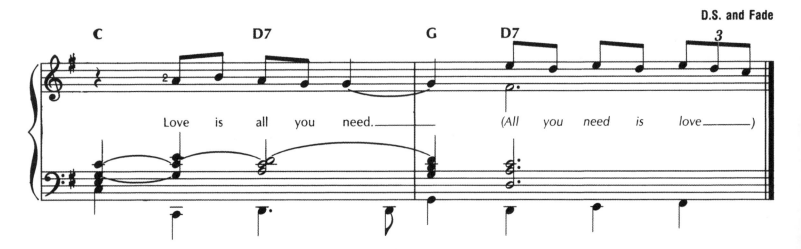

And I Love Her

Electronic Organs
Upper: Flutes (or Tibias) 16', 8'
       String 4'
Lower: Flute 8', Diapason 8', String 8'
Pedal: String Bass
Vib./Trem.: On, Fast

Tonebar Organs
Upper: 81 5505 004
Lower: (00) 7343 312
Pedal: String Bass
Vib./Trem.: On, Fast

Words and Music by John Lennon
and Paul McCartney

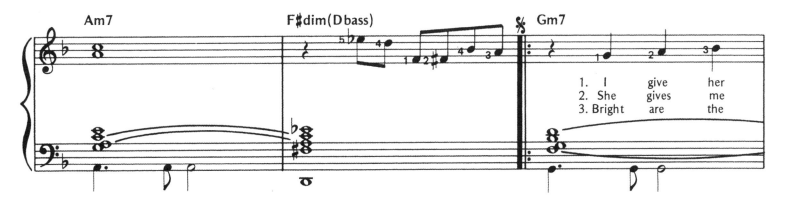

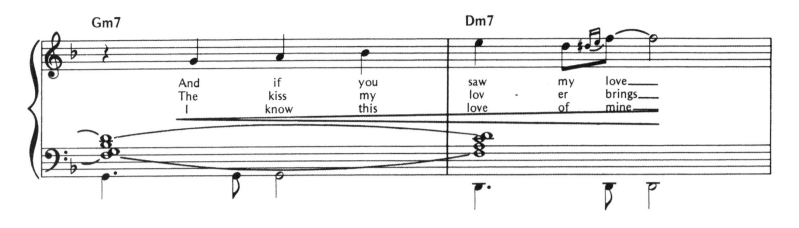

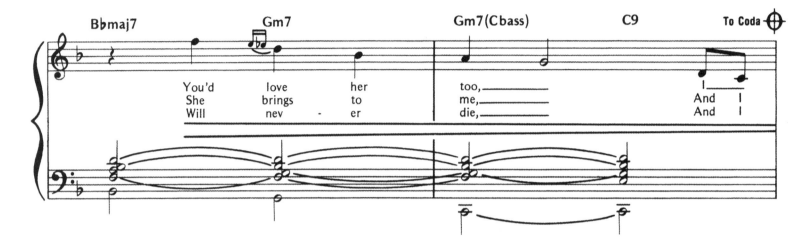

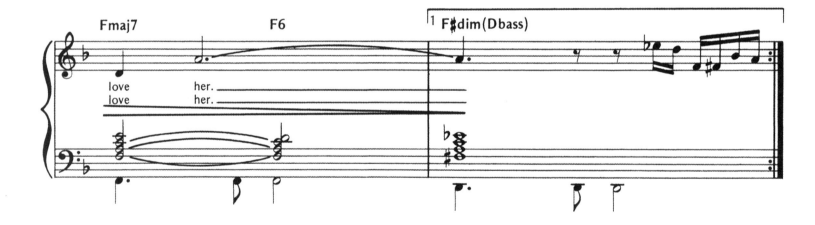

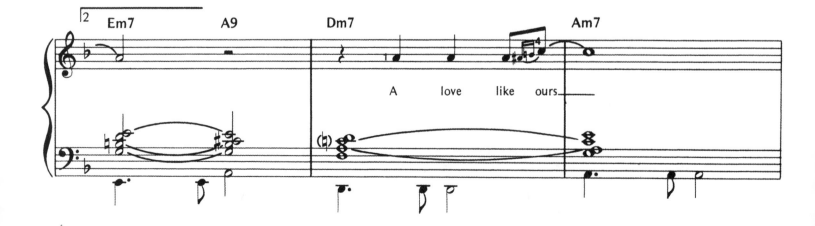

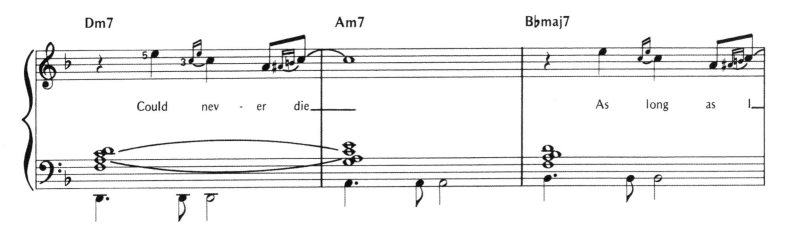

Dm7   Am7   B♭maj7

Could nev - er die___   As long as I___

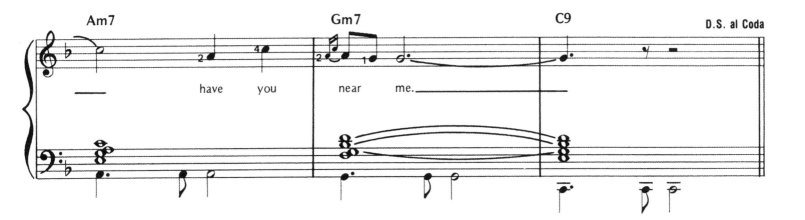

Am7   Gm7   C9   **D.S. al Coda**

have you   near me.___

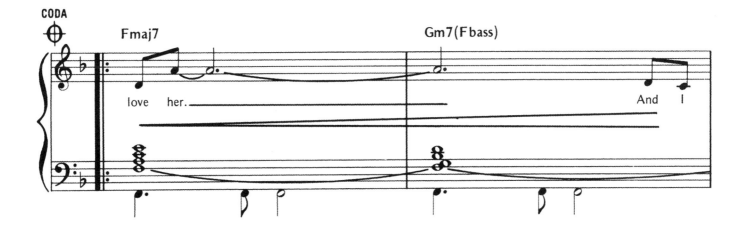

CODA

Fmaj7   Gm7(F bass)

love her.___   And I

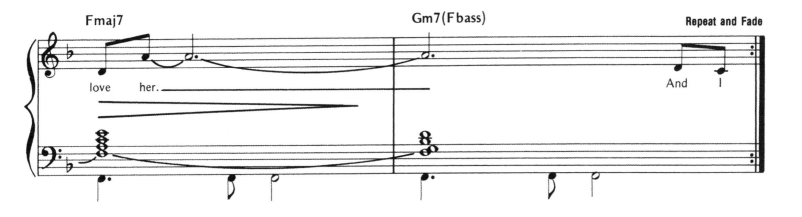

Fmaj7   Gm7(F bass)   **Repeat and Fade**

love her.___   And I

Can't Buy Me Love

Electronic Organs

Upper: Flutes (or Tibias) 16', 8', 4'
         String 8', Oboe, Trombone
Lower: Flute 8', Diapason 8',
         String 8', Reed 8'
Pedal: String Bass
Vib./Trem.: On, Fast

Tonebar Organs

Upper: 80 7003 051
Lower: (00) 7303 004
Pedal: String Bass
Vib./Trem.: On, Fast

Words and Music by John Lennon
and Paul McCartney

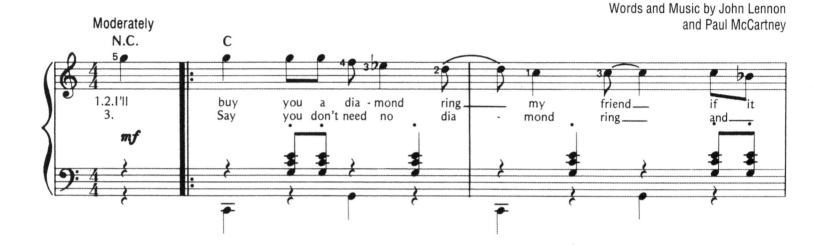

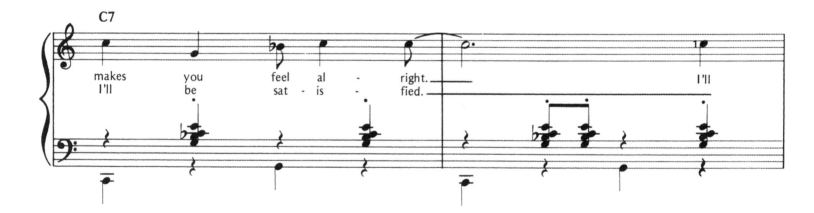

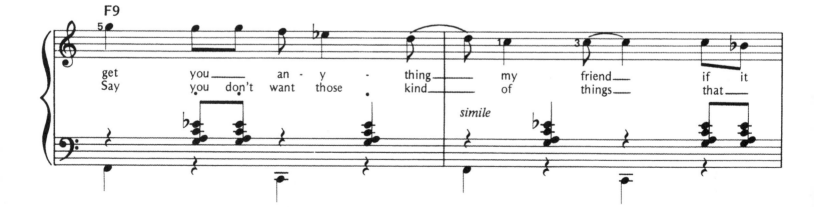

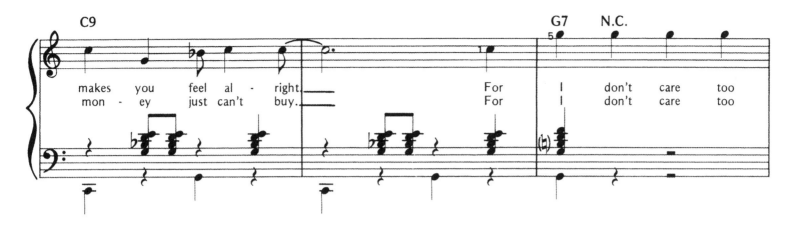

makes you feel al - right. _____ For I don't care too
mon - ey just can't buy. _____ For I don't care too

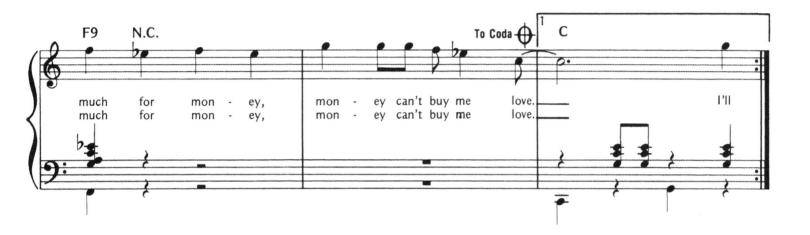

much for mon - ey, mon - ey can't buy me love. _____ I'll
much for mon - ey, mon - ey can't buy me love.

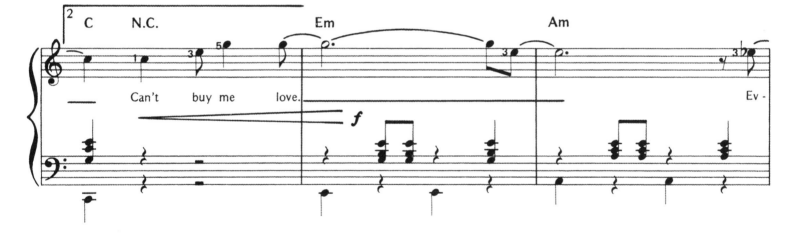

_____ Can't buy me love. _____ Ev -

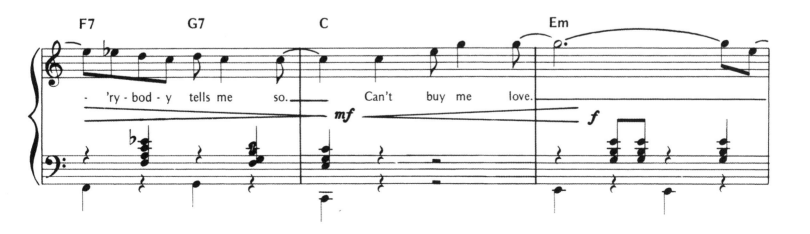

- 'ry - bod - y tells me so. _____ Can't buy me love. _____

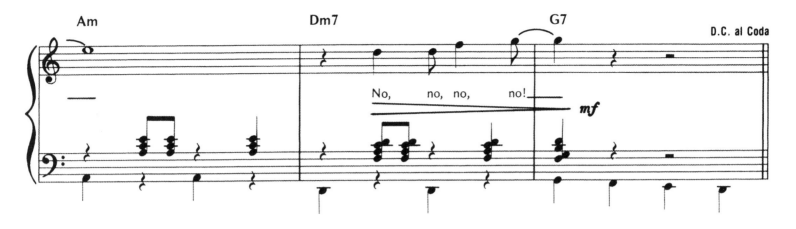

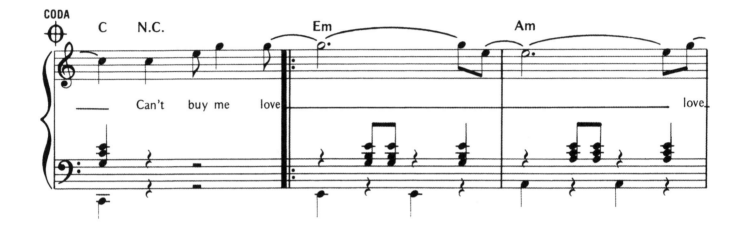

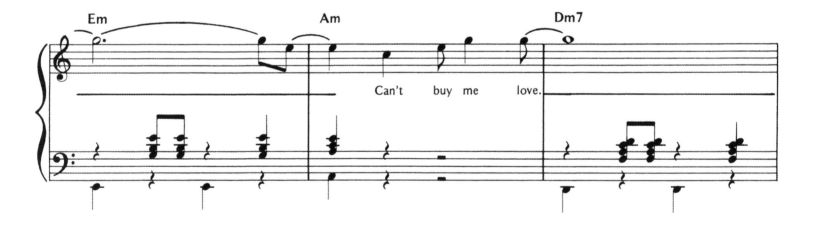

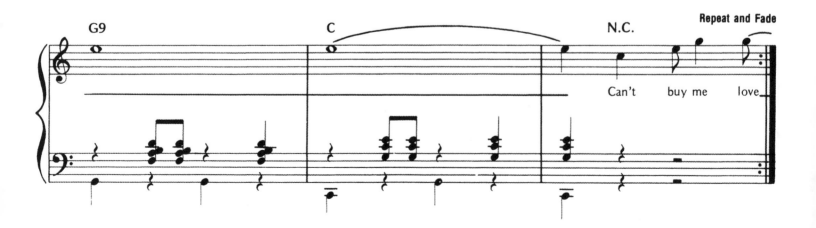

Come Together

Electronic Organs
Upper: Flutes (or Tibias) 16', 8', 4', 2'
         String 8'
Lower: Flutes 8', 4'
Pedal: 16', 8'
Vib./Trem.: On, Fast

Drawbar Organs
Upper: 80 8104 103
Lower: (00) 6303 004
Pedal: 34
Vib./Trem.: On, Fast

Words and Music by John Lennon
and Paul McCartney

Moderately slow, in 2

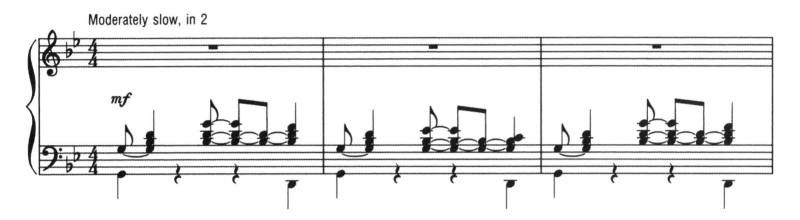

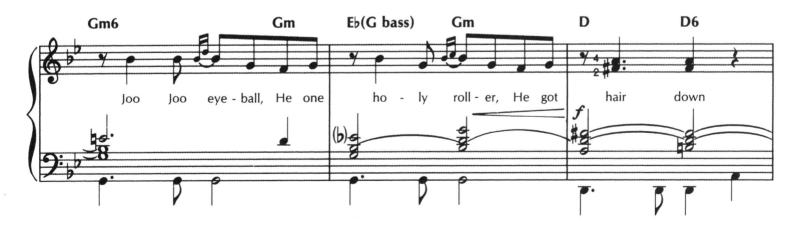

to his knee.__ Got to be a jok-er, He just do what he please.__

He wear no shoe-shine, He got to jam foot-ball, He got
He Bag Pro-duc-tion, He got wal-rus gum-boot, He got
He roll-er coast-er, He got ear-ly warn-ing, He got

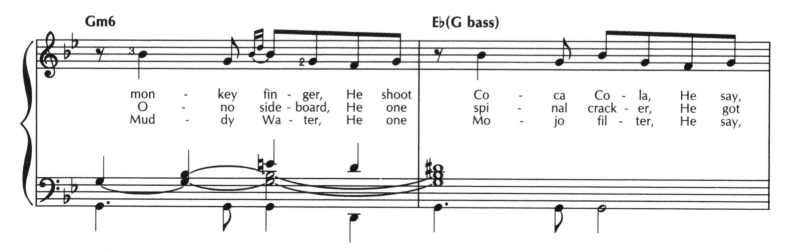

mon-key fin-ger, He shoot Co-ca Co-la, He say,
O-no side-board, He one spi-nal crack-er, He got
Mud-dy Wa-ter, He one Mo-jo fil-ter, He say,

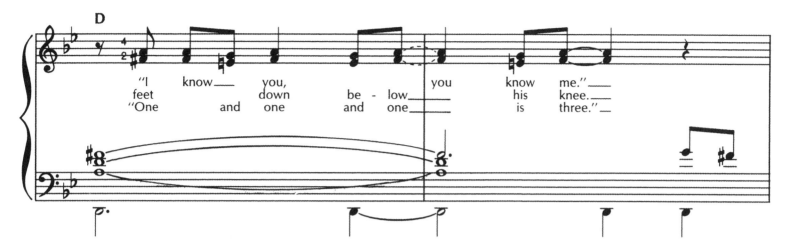

"I know___ you, you know me."___
feet down be - low___ you his knee.___
"One and one and one___ is three."___

C7   **C9**   **C7**   **Em**   **Em7(D bass)**

One thing I can tell you is you got to be free.___
Hold you in his arm - chair, you can feel his dis - ease.
Got to be good look - ing 'cause he so hard to see.___
Come to - geth - er,___ right

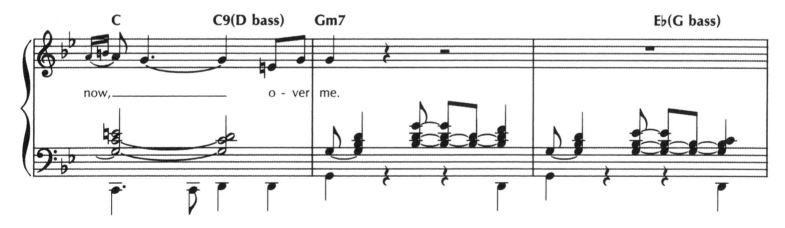

C   **C9(D bass)**   **Gm7**   **Eb(G bass)**

now,___ o - ver me.

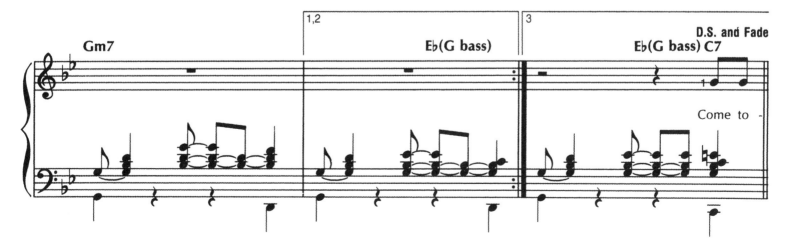

Gm7   **1,2 Eb(G bass)**   **3 D.S. and Fade** **Eb(G bass) C7**

Come to -

Day Tripper

Electronic Organs
Upper: Flutes (or Tibias) 16', 8', 4'
Lower: Piano, Melodia 8'
Pedal: String Bass
Vib./Trem.: On, Slow

Drawbar Organs
Upper: 80 7765 002
Lower: (00) 8076 000
Perc. attack
Pedal: String Bass
Vib./Trem.: On, Slow

Words and Music by John Lennon
and Paul McCartney

Driving rock tempo

for tak - ing the eas - y way out___ now.
she took me half___ the way there,___ now.
she on - ly played___ one night stands,___ now. She was a

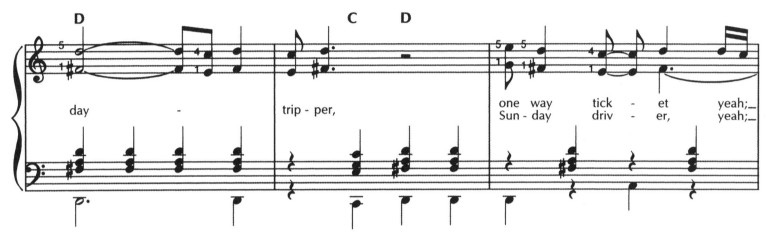

day - trip - per,
one way tick - et yeah;___
Sun - day driv - er, yeah;___

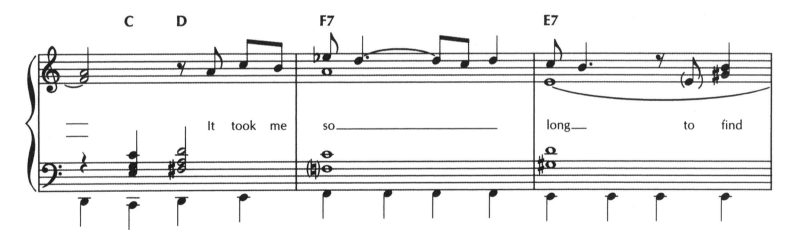

It took me so_____ long___ to find

out, and I found out.

out.

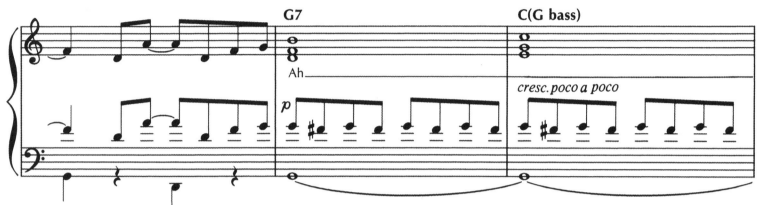

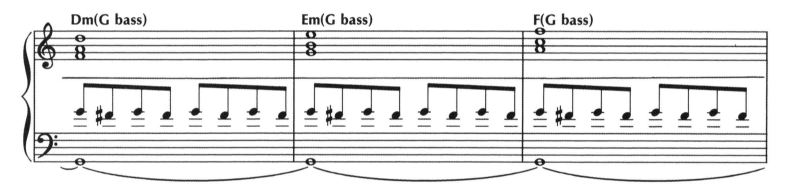

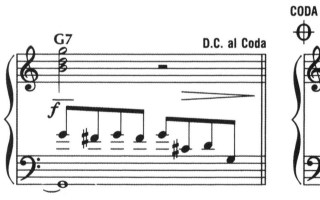

Eight Days A Week

Electronic Organs
Upper: Flutes (or Tibias) 16', 4'
       Trumpet, Oboe
Lower: Flute 4', Diapason 8', String 8'
Pedal: String Bass
Vib./Trem.: On, Fast

Tonebar Organs
Upper: 88 0808 088
Lower: (00) 8648 003
Pedal: String Bass
Vib./Trem.: On, Fast

Words and Music by John Lennon
and Paul McCartney

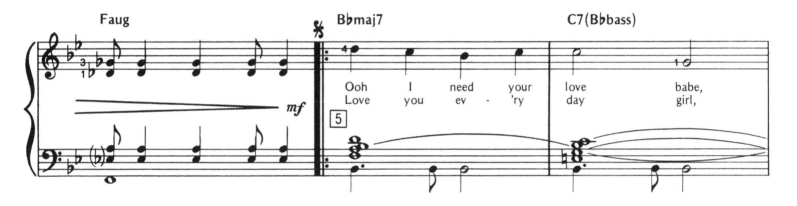

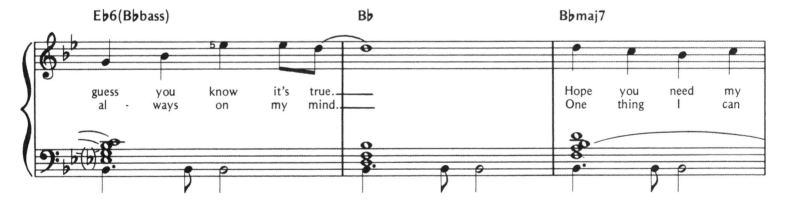

18

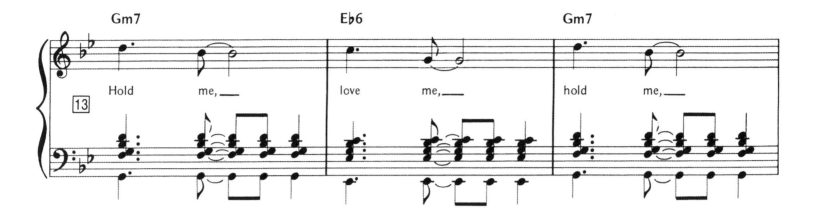

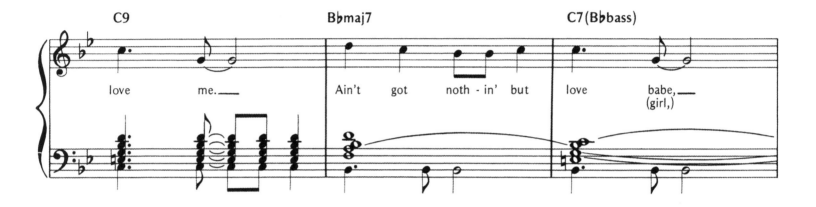

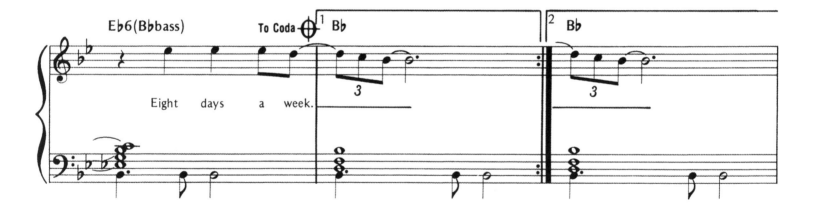

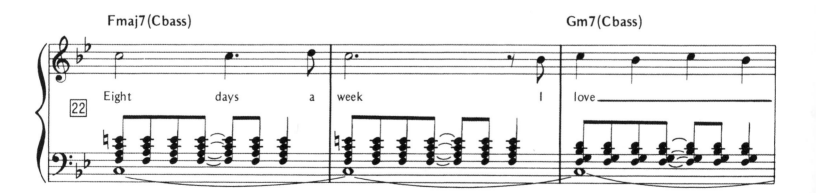

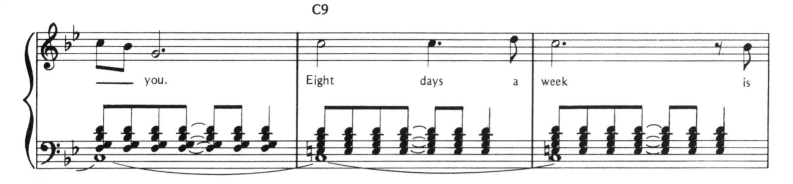

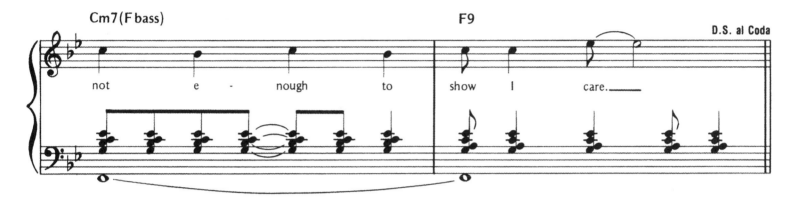

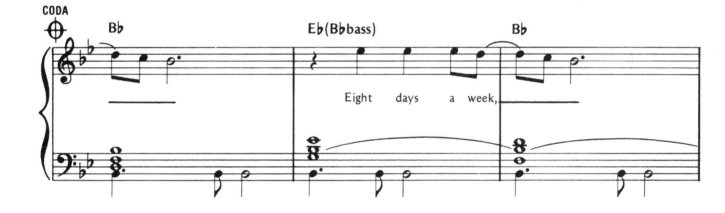

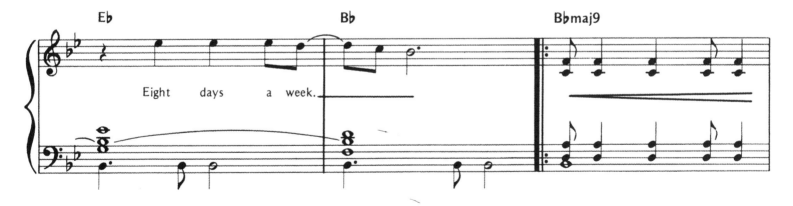

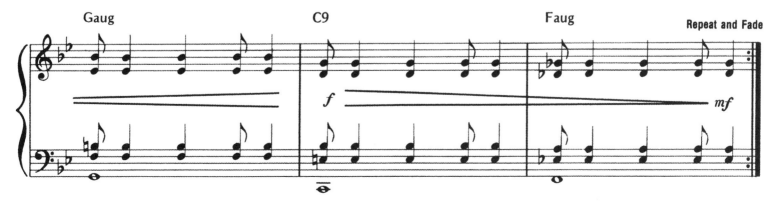

Eleanor Rigby

Electronic Organs
Upper: Flutes (or Tibias) 16', 8', 4', 2'
      String 8', 4'
Lower: Flutes 8', 4'
      String 8', 4'
Pedal: 16', 8'
Vib./Trem.: On, Fast

Tonebar Organs
Upper: 82 5325 004
Lower: (00) 7345 312
Pedal: 44
Vib./Trem.: On, Fast

Words and Music by John Lennon
and Paul McCartney

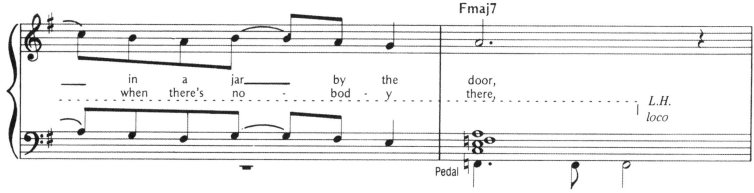

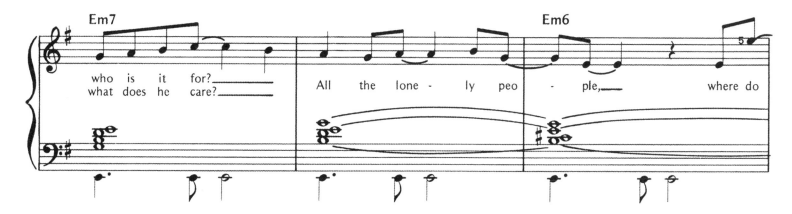

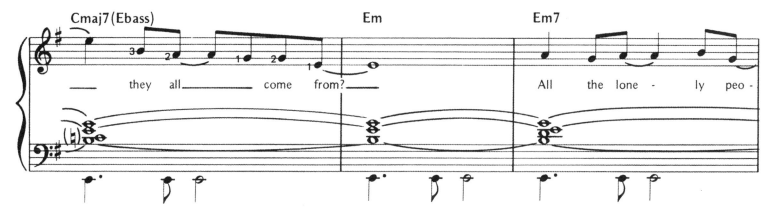

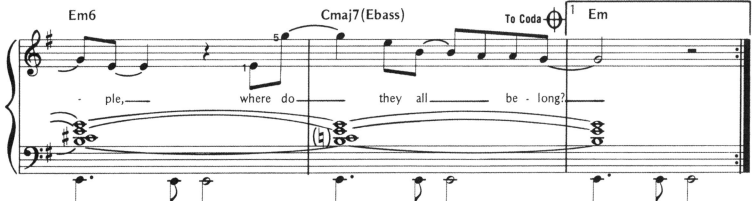

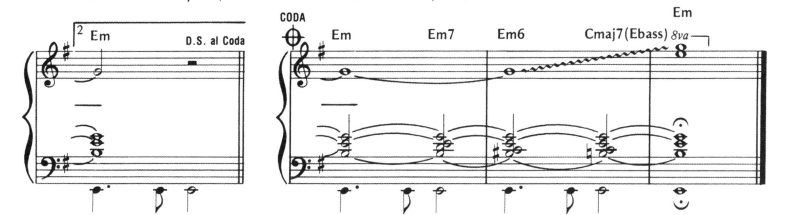

Get Back

Electronic Organs
Upper: Flutes (or Tibias) 16', 8', 5⅓', 4'
Lower: Flute 4', Diapason 8'
Pedal: String Bass
Vib./Trem.: On, Slow

Drawbar Organs
Upper: 85 0000 310
Lower: (00) 8401 005
Pedal: String Bass
Vib./Trem.: On, Slow

Words and Music by John Lennon
and Paul McCartney

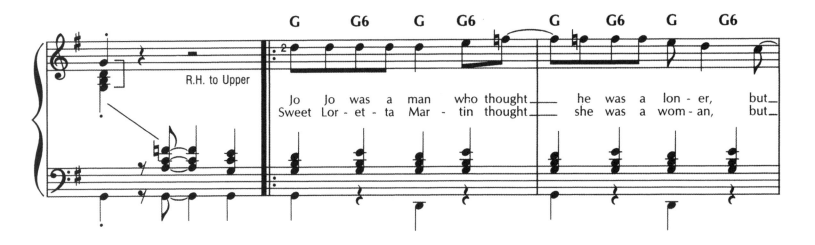

Jo Jo was a man who thought____ he was a lon-er, but
Sweet Lor-et-ta Mar-tin thought____ she was a wom-an, but

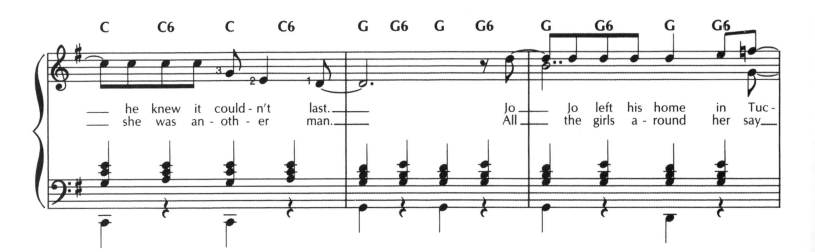

____ he knew it could-n't last.
she was an-oth-er man.

Jo ____ Jo left his home in Tuc-say
All ____ the girls a-round her say

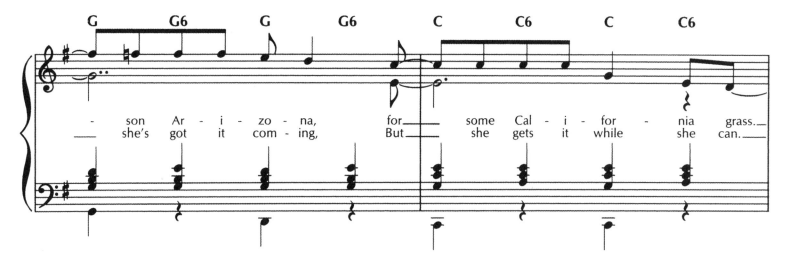

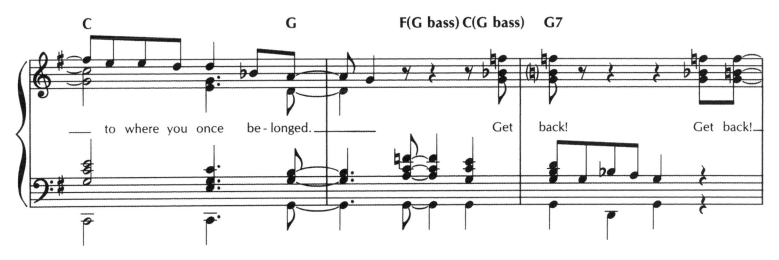

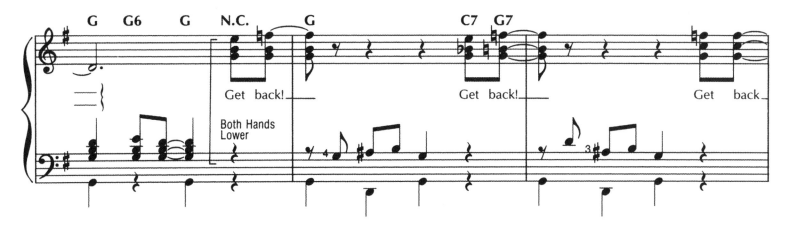

Upper: Fuzz or Acoustic Guitar

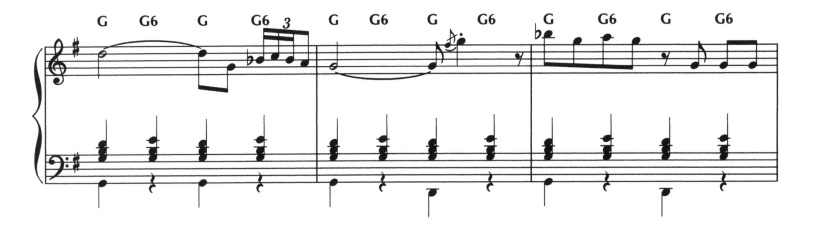

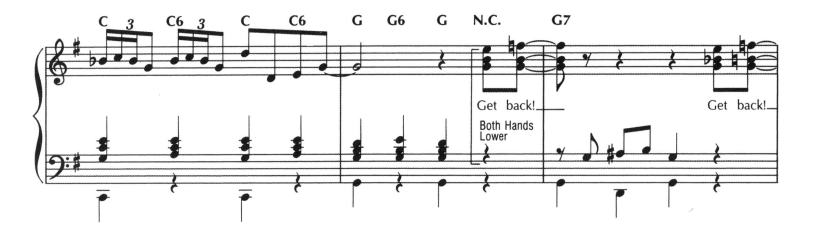

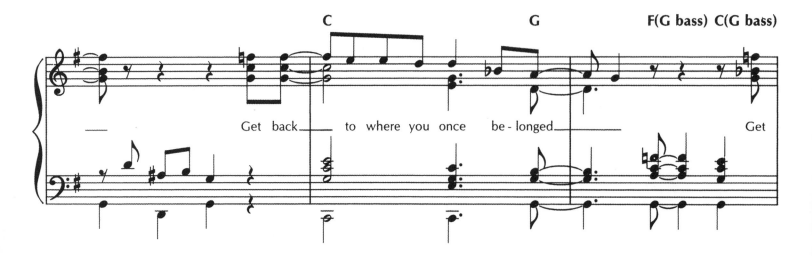

back! Get back! Get back to where you once be-longed.

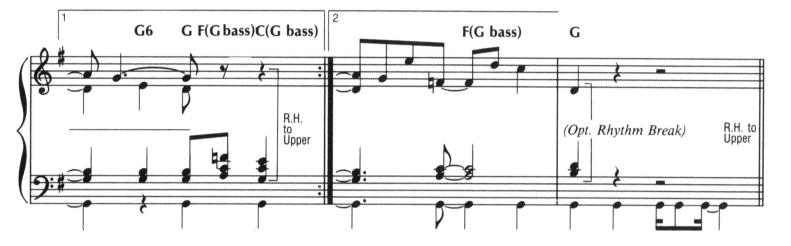

R.H. to Upper

(Opt. Rhythm Break) R.H. to Upper

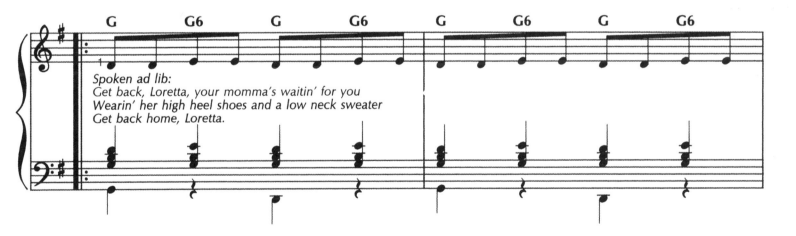

Spoken ad lib:
Get back, Loretta, your momma's waitin' for you
Wearin' her high heel shoes and a low neck sweater
Get back home, Loretta.

Repeat and Fade

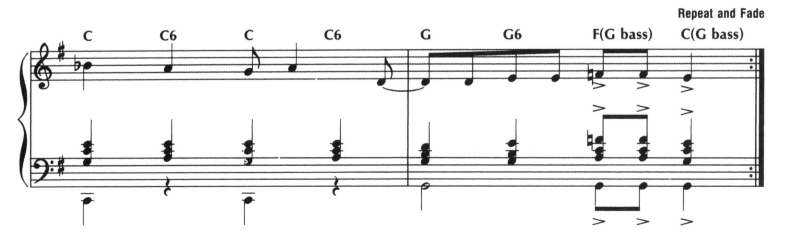

A Hard Day's Night

Electronic Organs
Upper: Preset Piano
Lower: Flutes 8', 4'
Pedal: String Bass
Vib./Trem.: On, Fast

Tonebar Organs
Upper: Preset Piano or
80 6606 000
Lower: (00) 7400 000
Pedal: 23
Vib./Trem.: On, Fast

Words and Music by John Lennon
and Paul McCartney

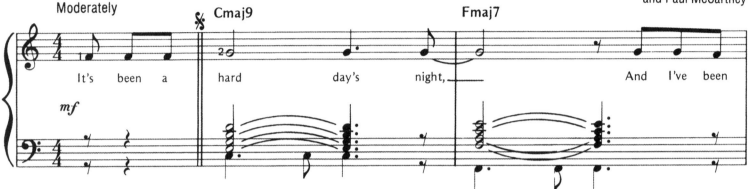

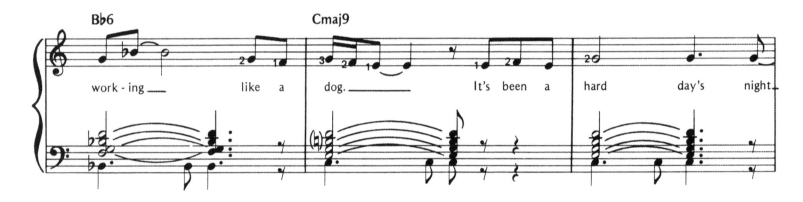

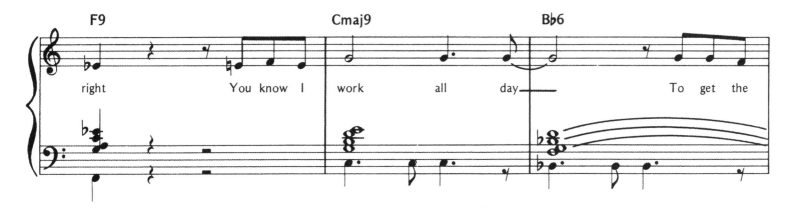

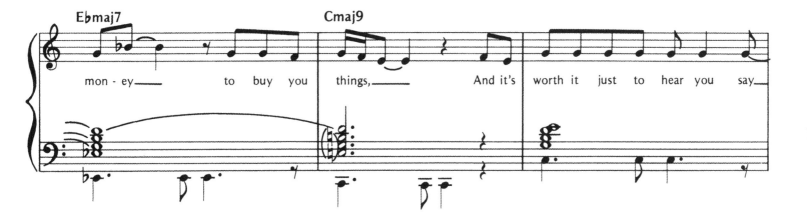

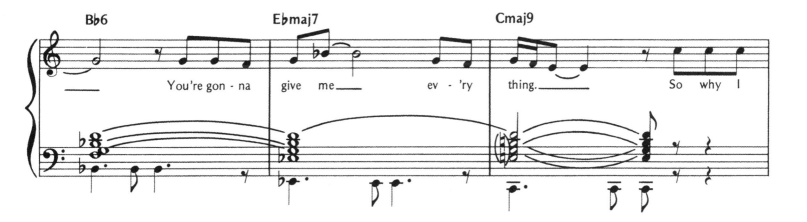

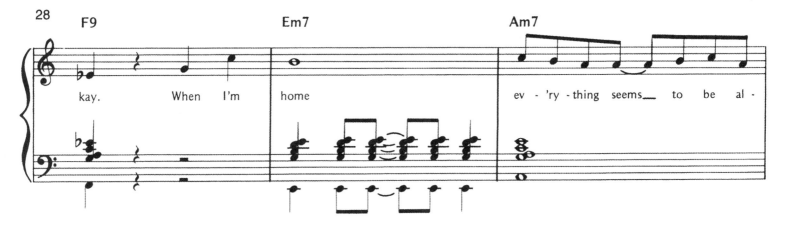

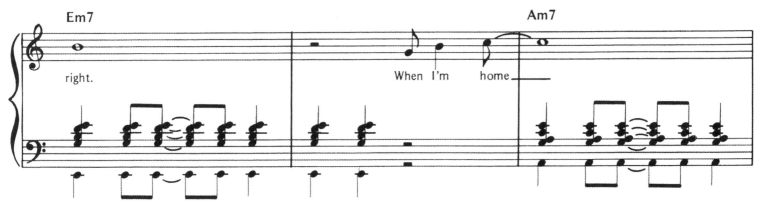

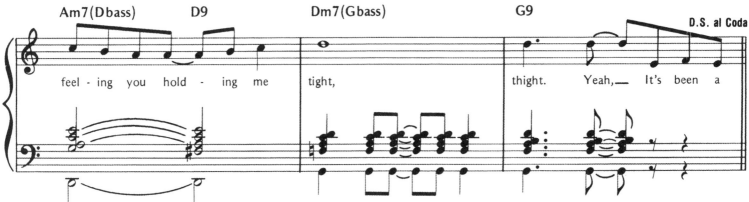

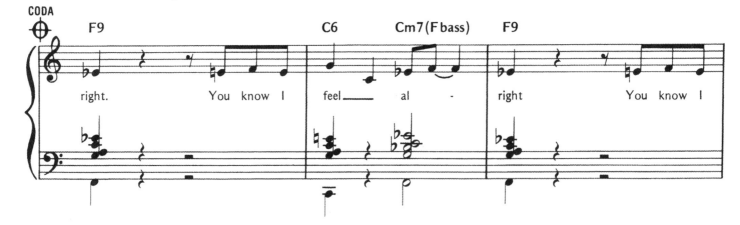

Hello, Goodbye

Electronic Organs
Upper: Flutes (or Tibias) 8', 4'
        String 8'
Lower: Reed 8', Melodia 8'
Pedal: 8'
Vib./Trem.: On, Fast

Drawbar Organs
Upper: 40 5536 001
Lower: (00) 7303 004
Pedal: 35
Vib./Trem.: On, Fast

Words and Music by John Lennon
and Paul McCartney

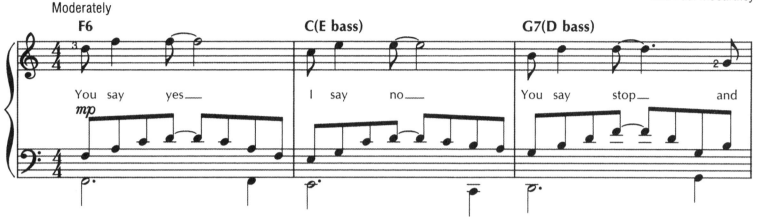

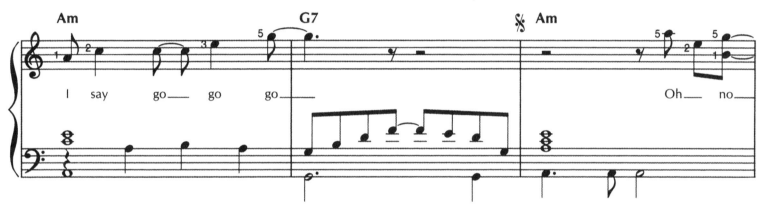

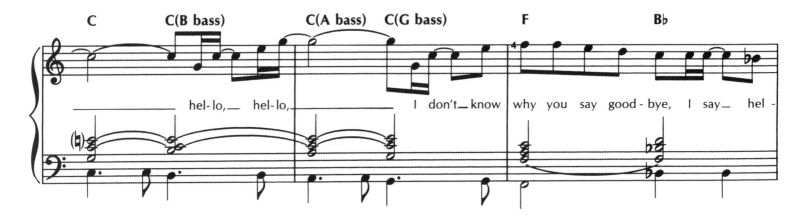

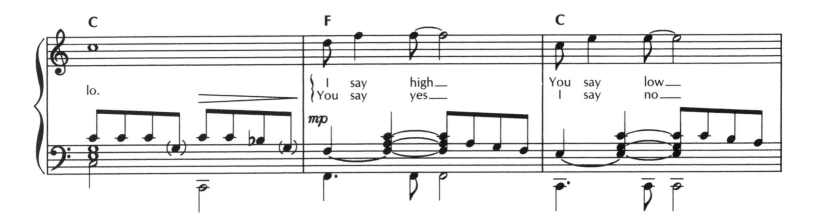

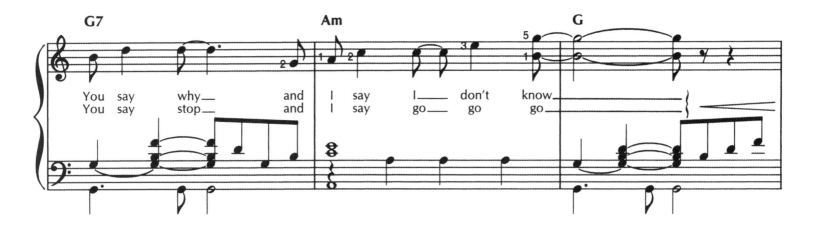

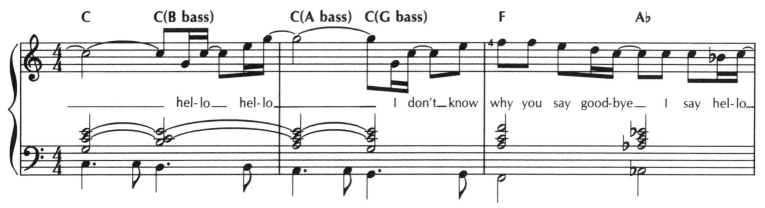

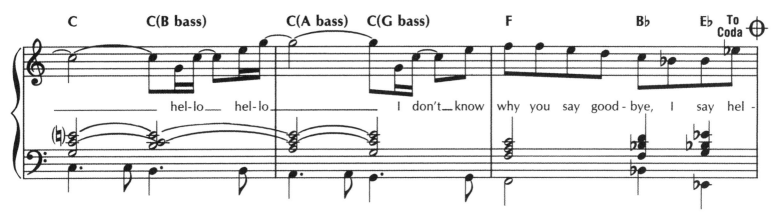

Hey Jude

Electronic Organs
Upper: Strings 8′, 4′
Lower: Melodia 8′
Pedal: 16′, 8′
Vib./Trem.: On, Fast

Drawbar Organs
Upper: 20 4800 012
Lower: (00) 7220 011
Pedal: 25
Vib./Trem.: On, Fast

Words and Music by John Lennon
and Paul McCartney

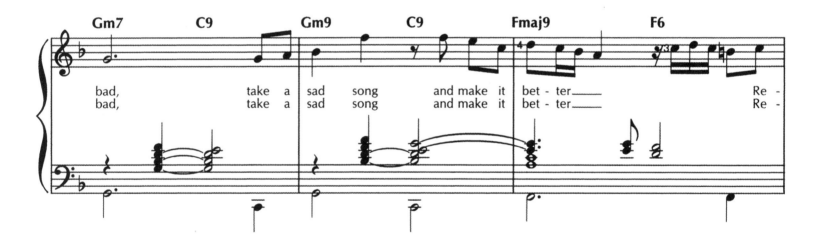

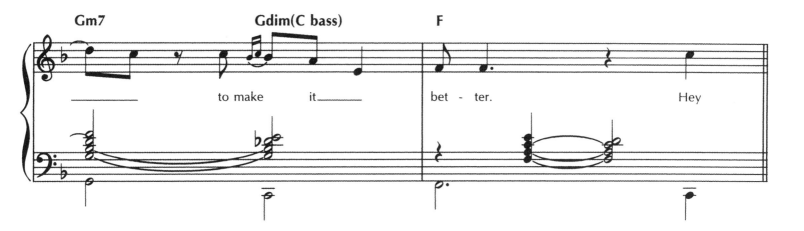

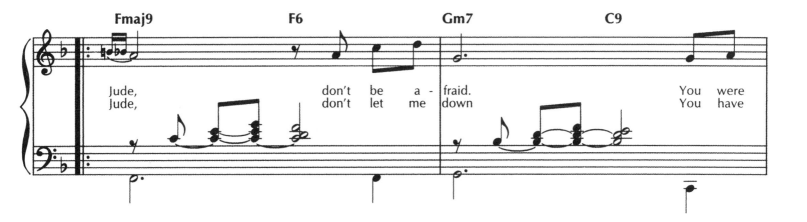

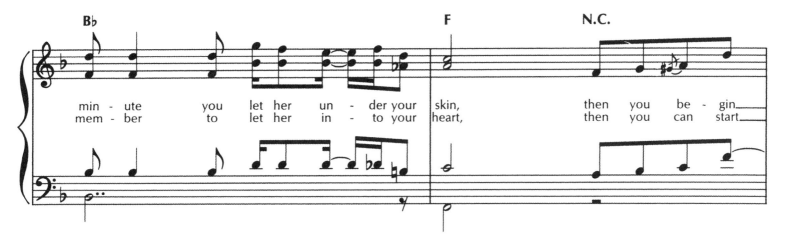

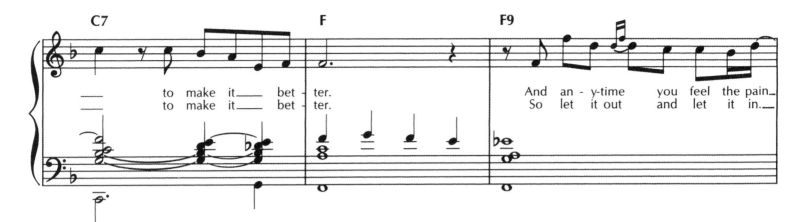

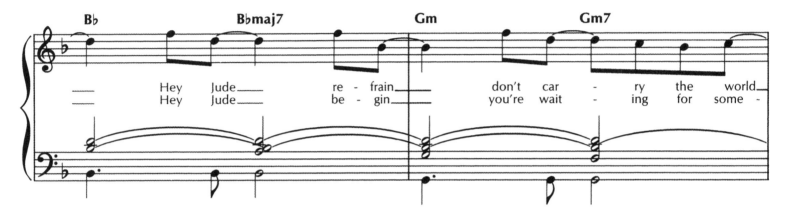

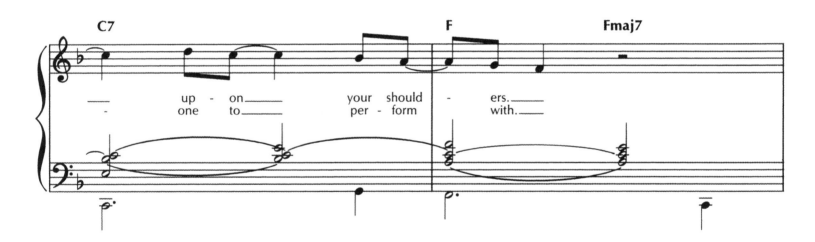

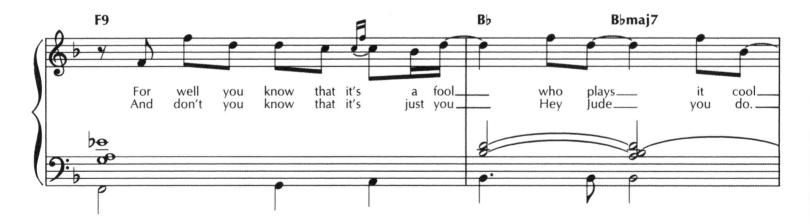

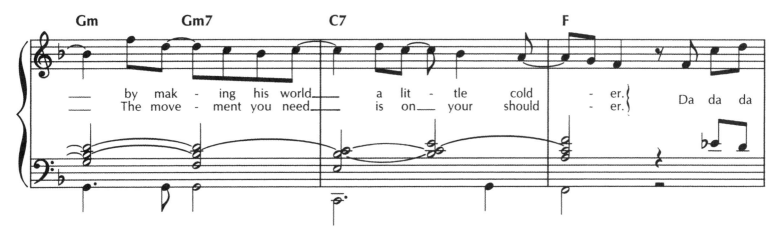

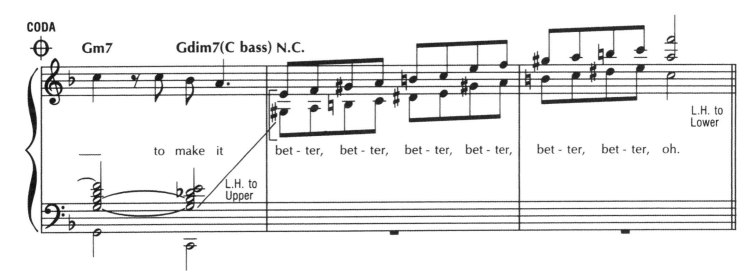

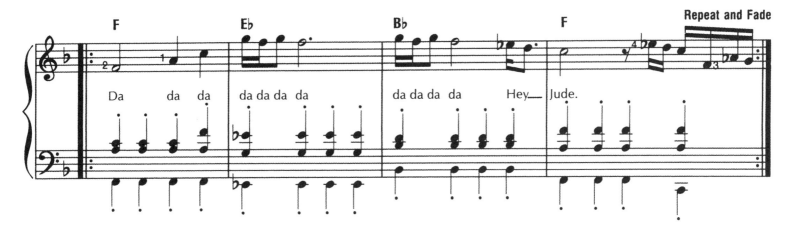

I Feel Fine

Electronic Organs
Upper: Flutes (or Tibias) 16', 2'
Lower: Flute 8', Reed 8'
Pedal: 8'
Vib./Trem.: On, Slow

Drawbar Organs
Upper: 40 0006 010
Lower: (00) 4014 000
Pedal: 34
Vib./Trem.: On, Slow

Words and Music by John Lennon
and Paul McCartney

Bright rock

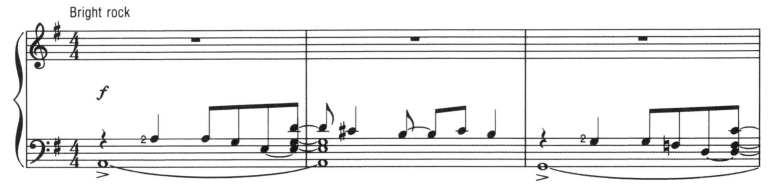

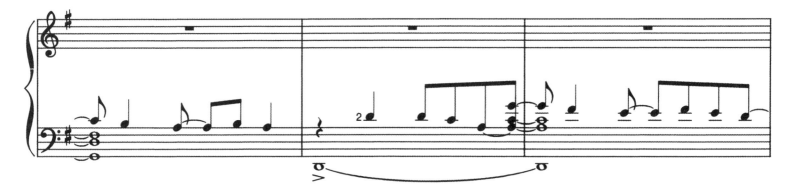

1.Ba - by's good to me, ____ you know, ____ she's
2,3.Ba - by says she's mine, ____ you know, ____ she

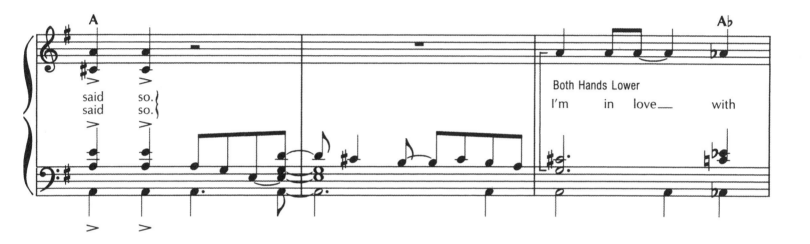

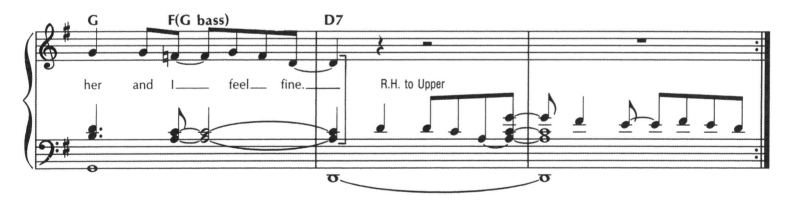

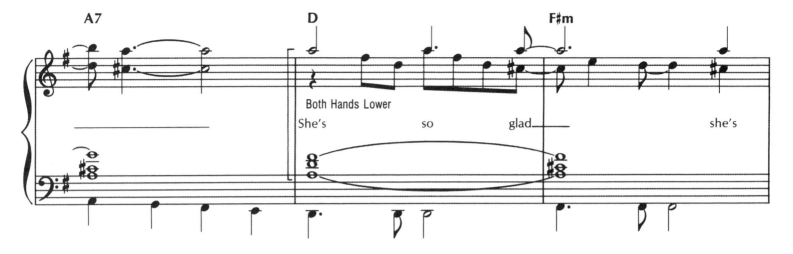

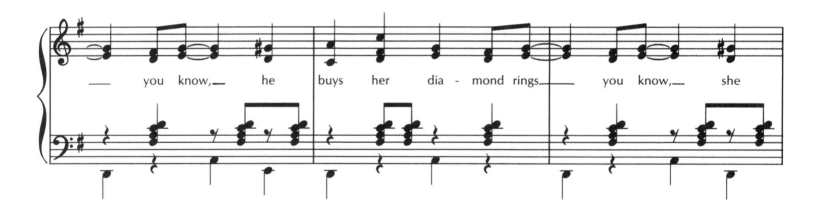

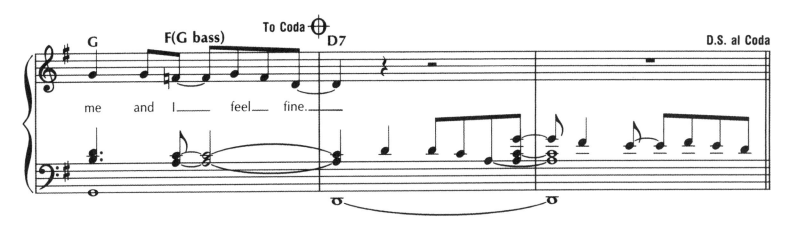

me and I___ feel___ fine..

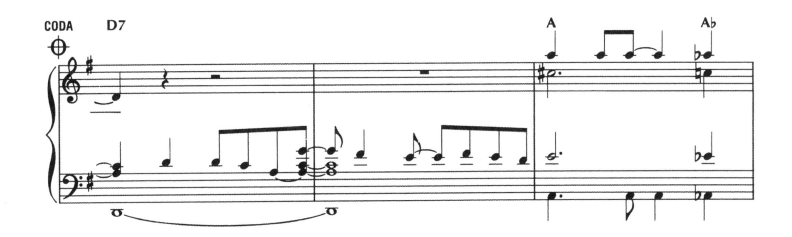

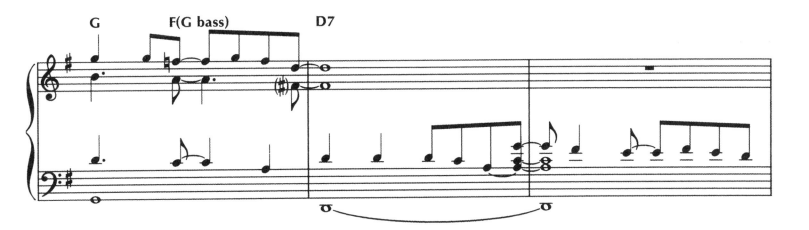

Help!

Electronic Organs
Upper: Flutes (or Tibias) 16′, 8′, 4′, 2′
Lower: Flutes 8′, 4′, Diapason 8′
Pedal: String Bass
Vib./Trem.: On, Fast

Drawbar Organs
Upper: 80 6606 000
Lower: (00) 7401 010
Pedal: String Bass
Vib./Trem.: On, Fast

Words and Music by John Lennon
and Paul McCartney

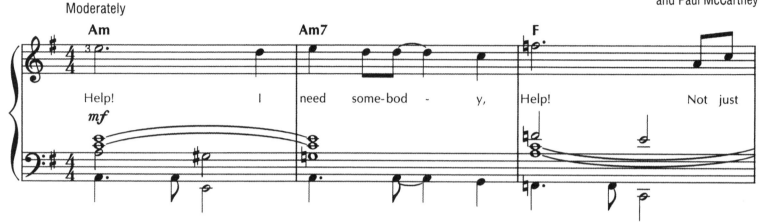

Moderately

Help! I need some-bod-y, Help! Not just

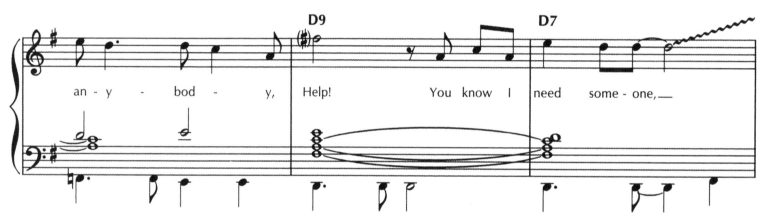

an-y-bod-y, Help! You know I need some-one,

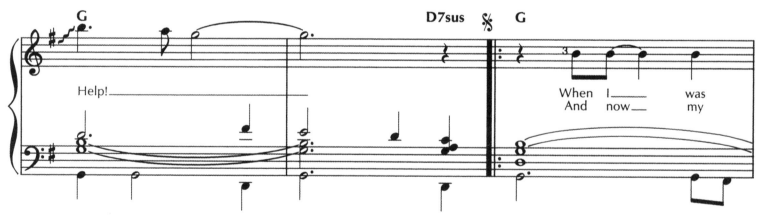

Help! When I was
And now my

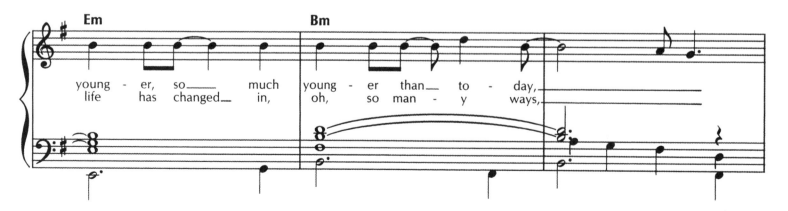

young-er, so much young-er than to-day,
life has changed much in, oh, so man-y ways,

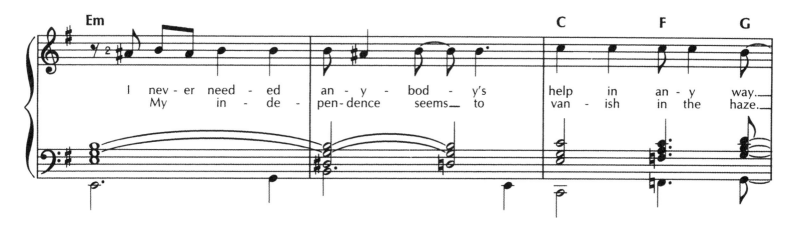

I nev-er need-ed an-y-bod-y's help in an-y way.
My in-de-pen-dence seems to van-ish in the haze.

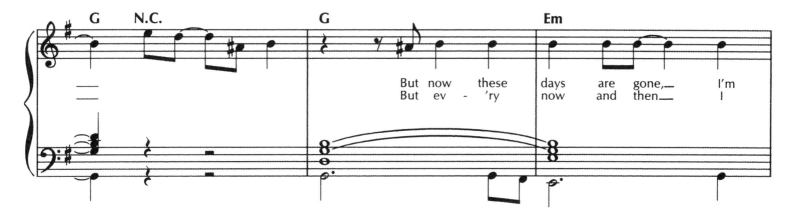

But now these days are gone,___ I'm
But ev-'ry now and then___ I

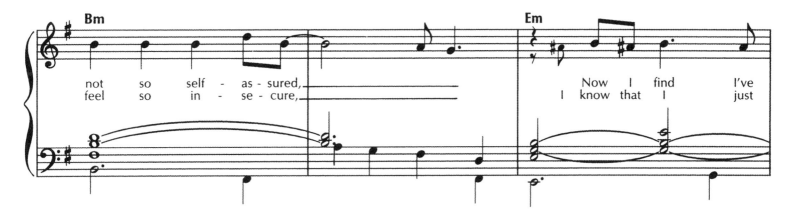

not so self-as-sured,___
feel so in-se-cure,___
Now I find I've
I know that I just

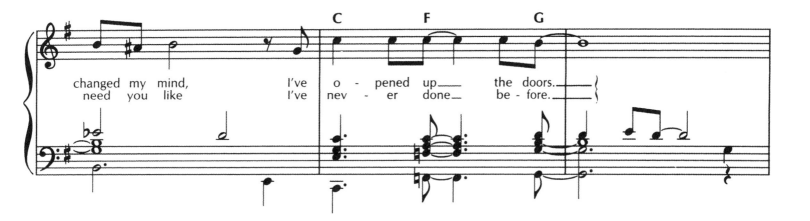

changed my mind, I've o-pened up___ the doors.___
need you like I've nev-er done___ be-fore.___

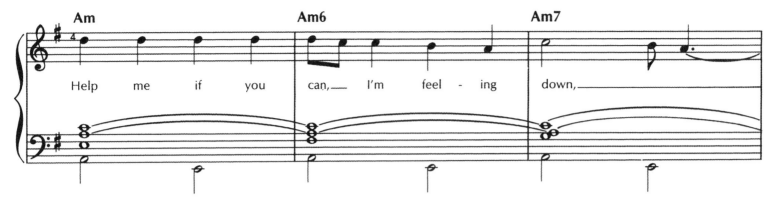

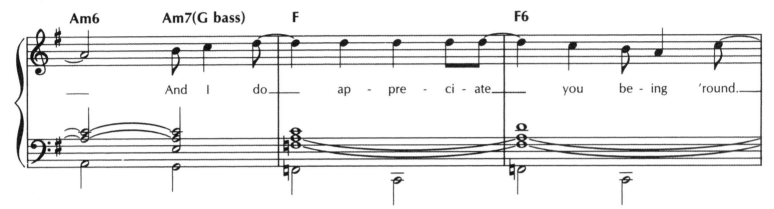

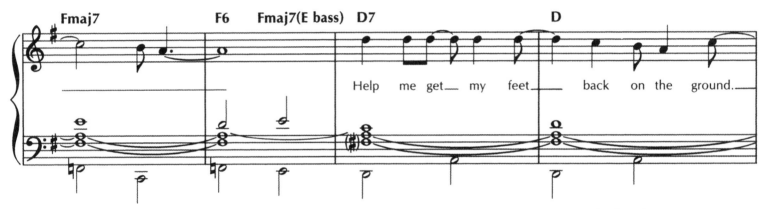

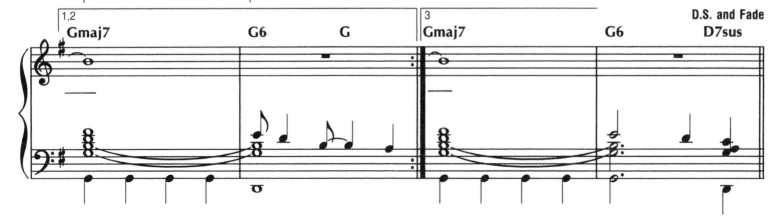

I Want To Hold Your Hand

Electronic Organs

Upper: Flutes (or Tibias) 16', 8', 4', 2',
       Trumpet, Clarinet
Lower: Flutes 8', 4', Strings 8', 4',
       Reed 8'
Pedal: 16', 8'
Vib./Trem.: On, Fast

Tonebar Organs

Upper: 83 0313 003
Lower: (00) 6303 002
Pedal: 04
Vib./Trem.: On, Fast

Words and Music by John Lennon
and Paul McCartney

Moderato (with a beat)

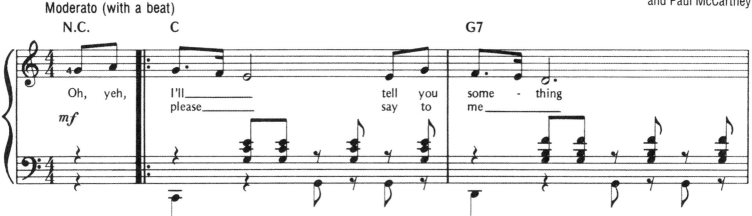

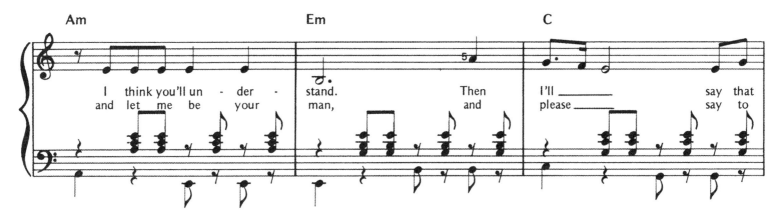

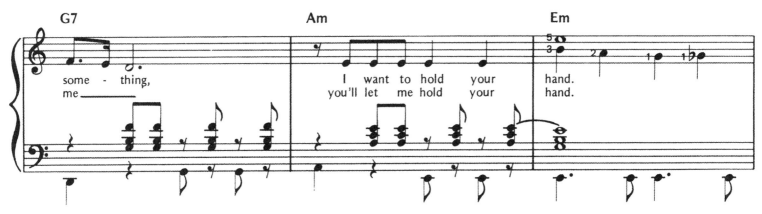

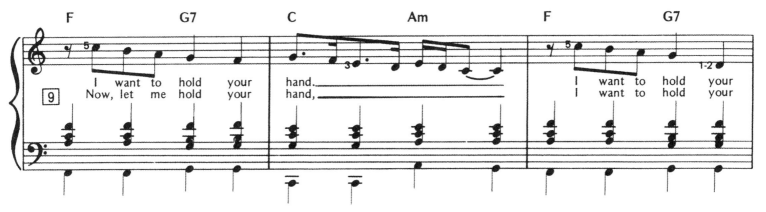

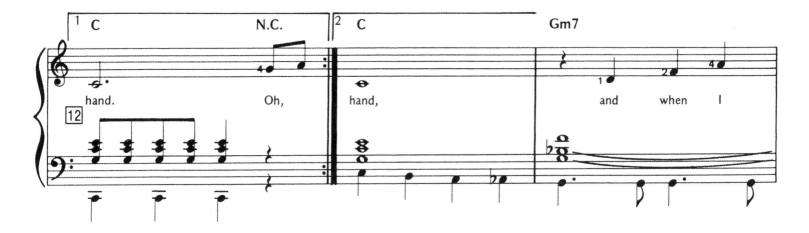

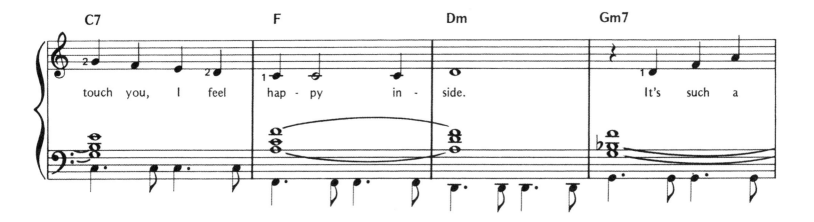

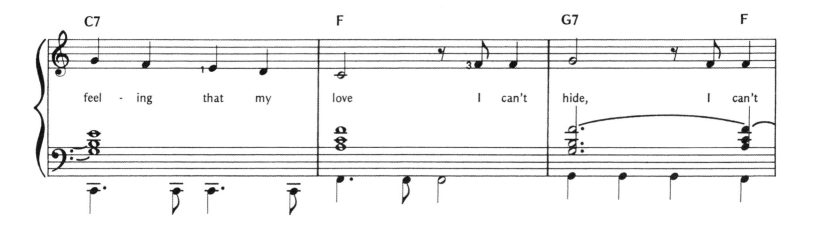

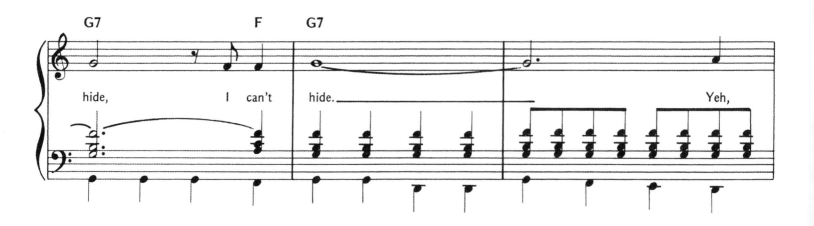

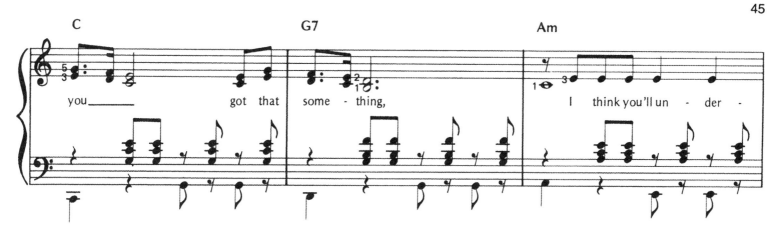

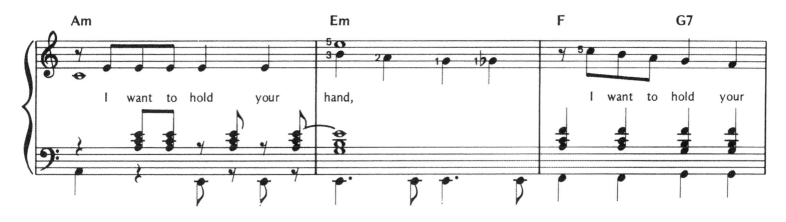

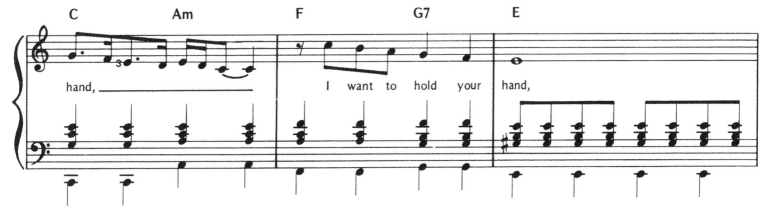

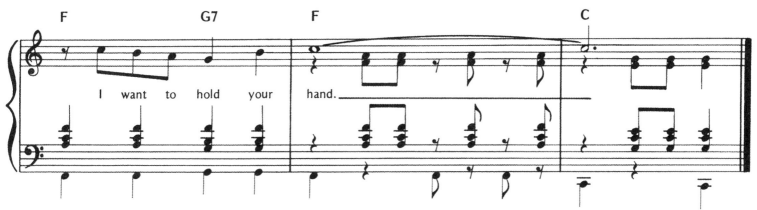

Lady Madonna

Electronic Organs
Upper: Flutes (or Tibias) 16', 4'
    Add Percuss
Lower: Flutes 8', 4'
Pedal: String Bass
Vib./Trem.: On, Slow

Drawbar Organs
Upper: 80 0400 311
    Add Percuss
Lower: (00) 7404 203
Pedal: String Bass
Vib./Trem.: On, Slow

Words and Music by John Lennon
and Paul McCartney

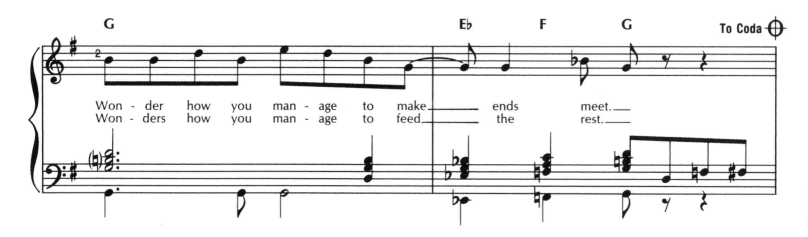

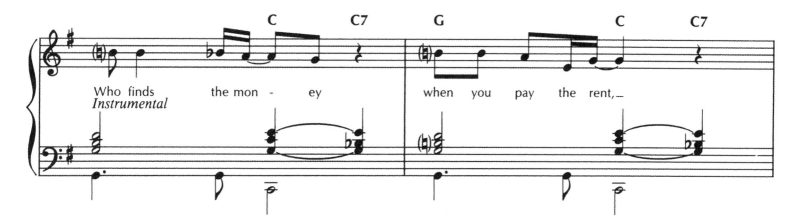

Who finds the mon — ey when you pay the rent,
Instrumental

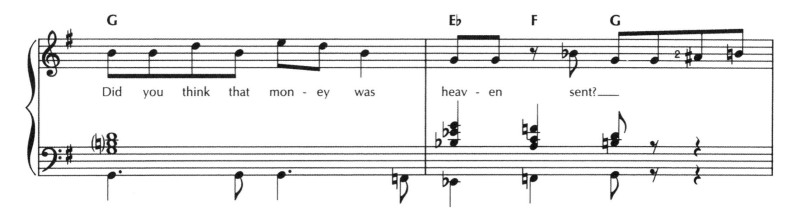

Did you think that mon — ey was heav — en sent?

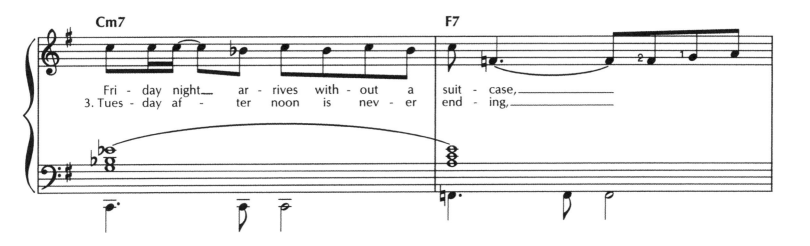

Fri - day night ar - rives with - out a suit - case,
3. Tues - day af - ter noon is nev - er end - ing,

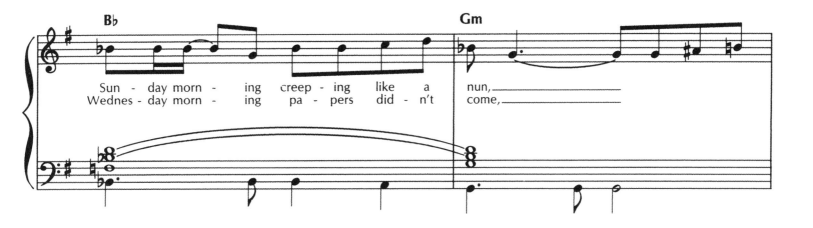

Sun - day morn — ing creep - ing like a nun,
Wednes - day morn — ing pa - pers did - n't come,

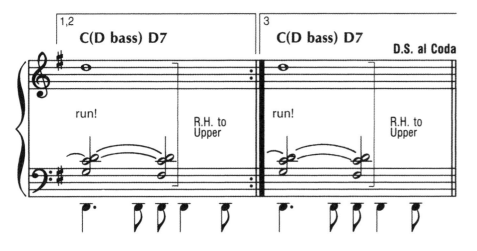

Additional Lyrics

3. Lady Madonna, lying on the bed.
Listen to the music playing in your head.
Instrumental
Tuesday afternoon is never ending,
Wednesday morning papers didn't come,
Thursday night your stockings needed mending.

4. Lady Madonna, children at your feet,
Wonder how you manage to make ends meet.
Coda

Let It Be

Electronic Organs
Upper: Flutes (or Tibias) 16', 8', 4'
Lower: Melodia 8', Reed 8'
Pedal: 8'
Vib./Trem.: On, Fast

Tonebar Organs
Upper: 80 4800 000
Lower: (00) 7334 011
Pedal: 05
Vib./Trem.: On, Fast

Words and Music by John Lennon
and Paul McCartney

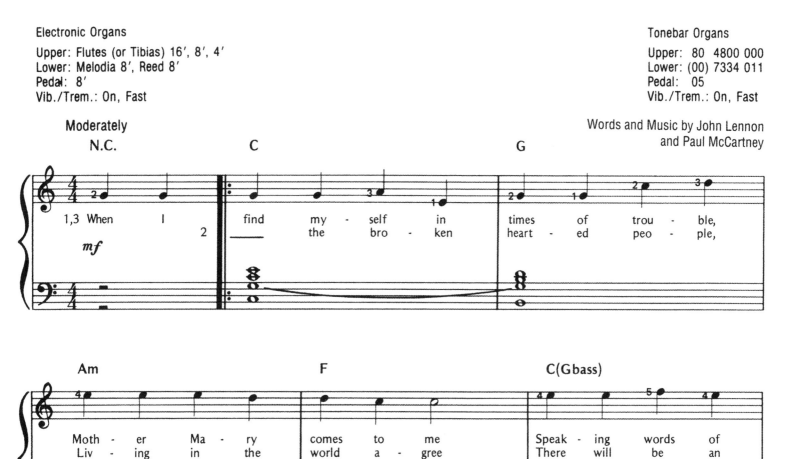

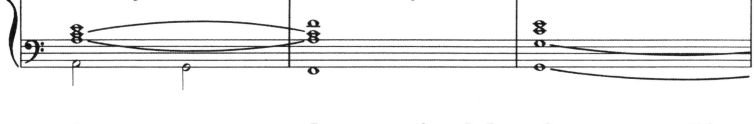

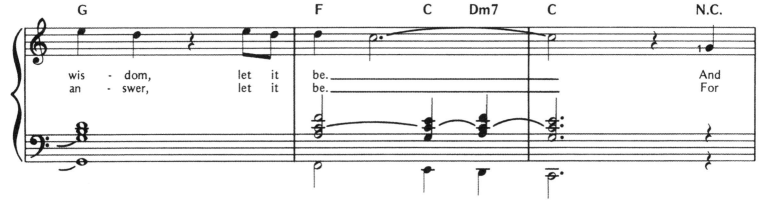

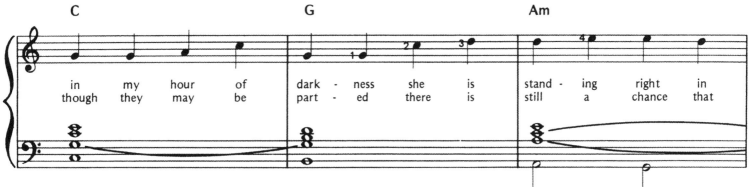

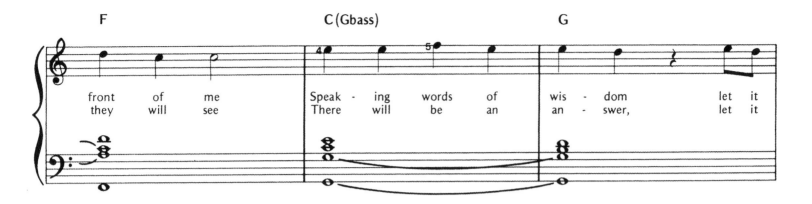

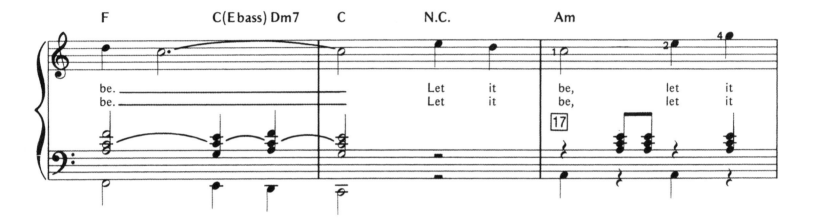

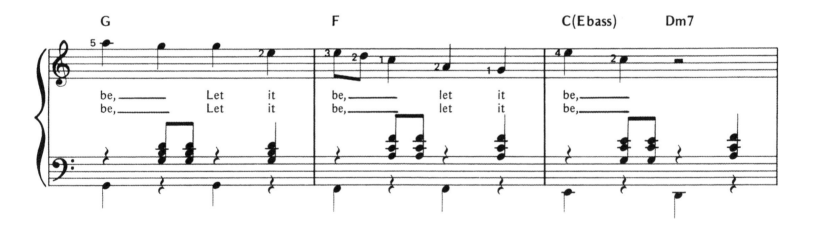

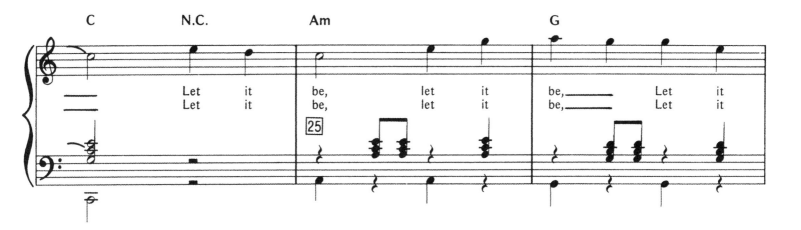

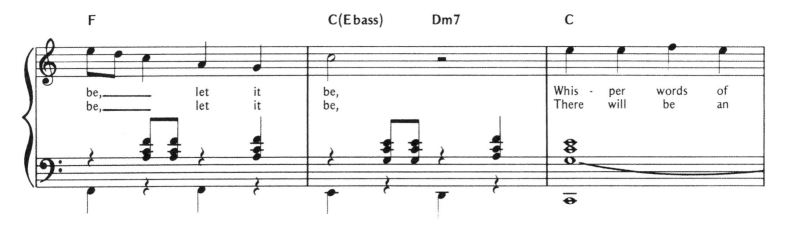

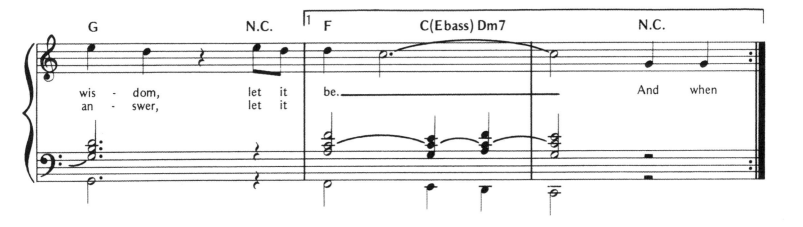

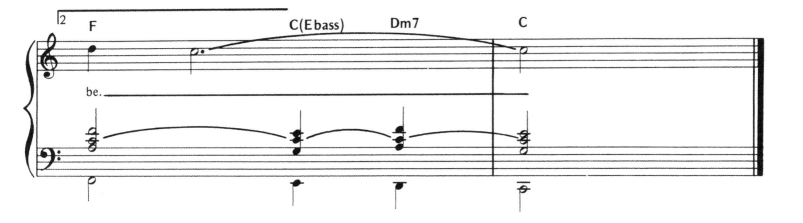

The Long And Winding Road

Electronic Organs
Upper: Flutes (or Tibias) 16′, 8′, 4′, 2′
        Trumpet, Clarinet
Lower: Flutes 8′, 4′
        Strings 8′, 4′, Reed 8′
Pedal: 16′, 8′
Vib./Trem.: On, Fast

Tonebar Organs
Upper: 83 0313 003
Lower: (00) 6303 002
Pedal: 04
Vib./Trem.: On, Fast

Words and Music by John Lennon
and Paul McCartney

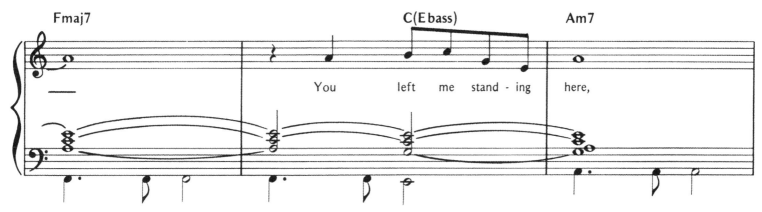

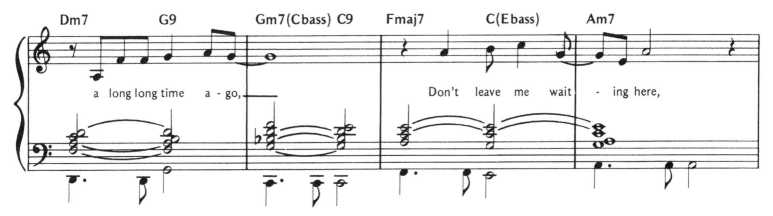

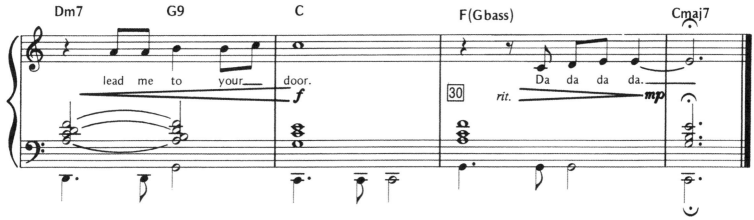

Love Me Do

Electronic Organs
Upper: Flutes (or Tibias) 16', 8', 5⅓', 4'
Lower: Flute 8', Diapason 8'
Pedal: String Bass
Vib./Trem.: On, Slow

Drawbar Organs
Upper: 85 0010 355
Add Perc
Lower: (00) 8401 007
Pedal: String Bass
Vib./Trem.: On, Slow

Words and Music by John Lennon
and Paul McCartney

Driving beat

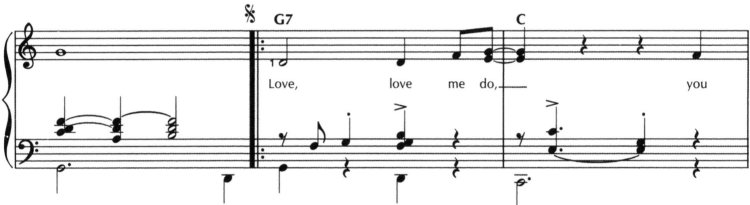

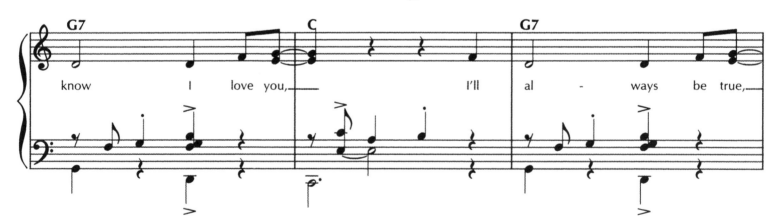

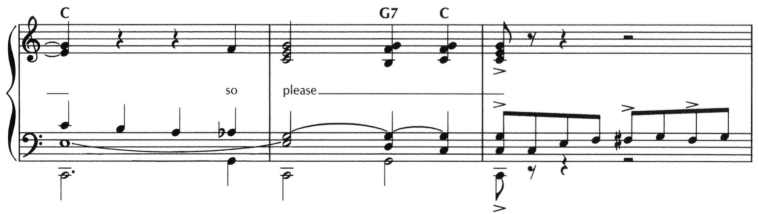

love me do._____ Woh,_____ love

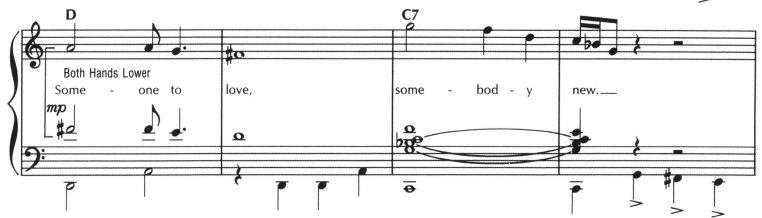

_____ me do._____

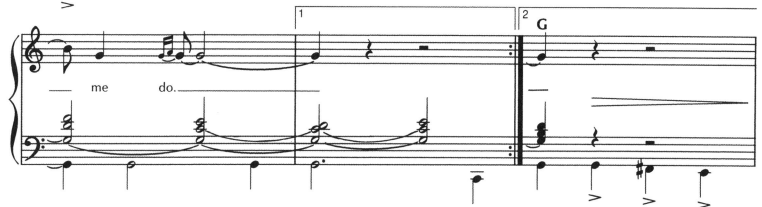

Both Hands Lower
Some - one to love, some - bod - y new._____

Some - one to love, some - one like you._____

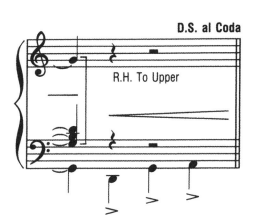

D.S. al Coda
R.H. To Upper

CODA
Repeat and Fade
Woh,_____ love_____ me do._____

Michelle

Electronic Organs
Upper: Flutes (or Tibias) 8′, 5⅓′, 4′, 2′
Lower: Flutes 8′, 4′, Diapason 8′,
     Reed 8′
Pedal: 16′, 8′
Vib./Trem.: On, Fast

Tonebar Organs
Upper: 86 6606 000
Lower: (00) 7732 211
Pedal: 55
Vib./Trem.: On, Fast

Words and Music by John Lennon
and Paul McCartney

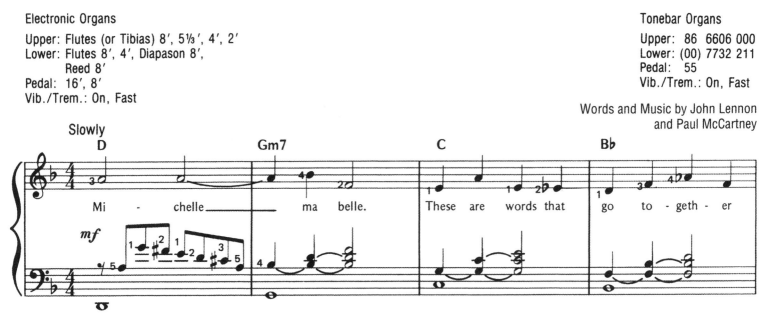

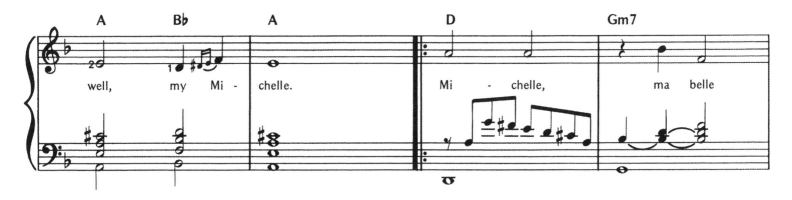

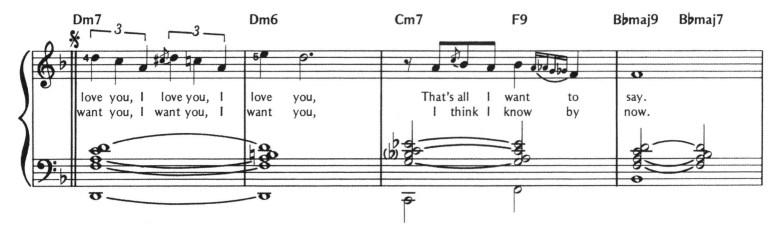

Until I find a way____ I will say the only words I know that
I'll get to you some-how.____ Un-til I do, I'm tell-ing you, so

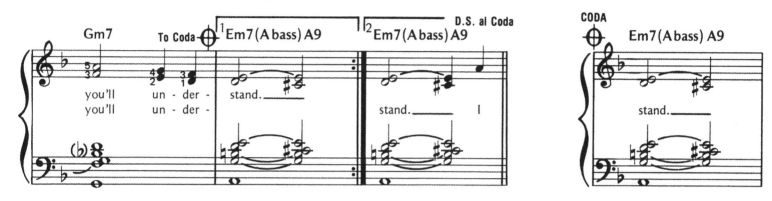

you'll un-der-stand.____
you'll un-der-stand. I

CODA

stand.____

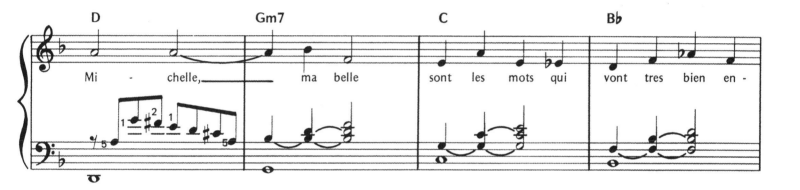

Mi-chelle,____ ma belle sont les mots qui vont tres bien en-

semble. tres bien en-semble. I will say the on-ly words I know that

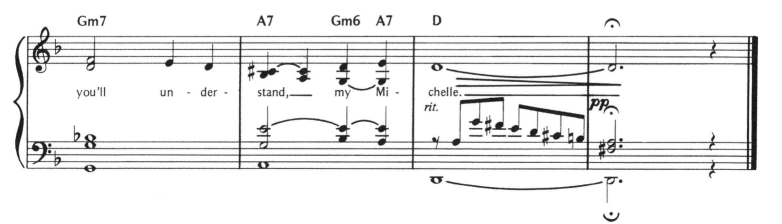

you'll un-der-stand,____ my Mi-chelle.____

Penny Lane

Electronic Organs
Upper: Flutes (or Tibias) 16', 8', 4', 2'
        Strings 8', 4', Trumpet
Lower: Flutes 8', 4', Strings 8', 4'
        Reed 8'
Pedal: 16', 8'
Vib./Trem.: On, Fast

Tonebar Organs
Upper: 80 7105 123
Lower: (00) 7314 003
Pedal: 25
Vib./Trem.: On, Fast

Words and Music by John Lennon
and Paul McCartney

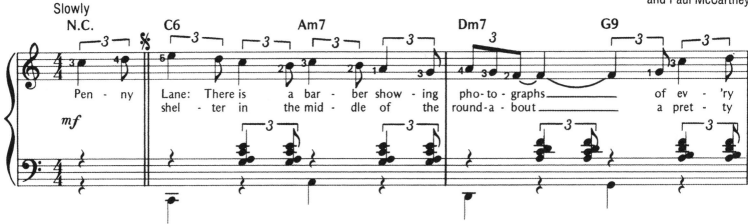

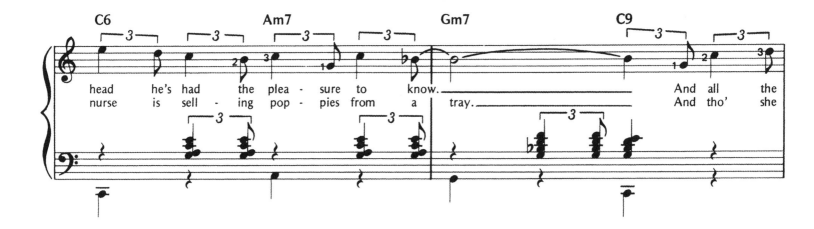

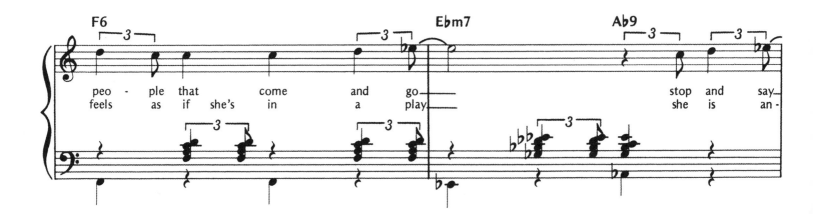

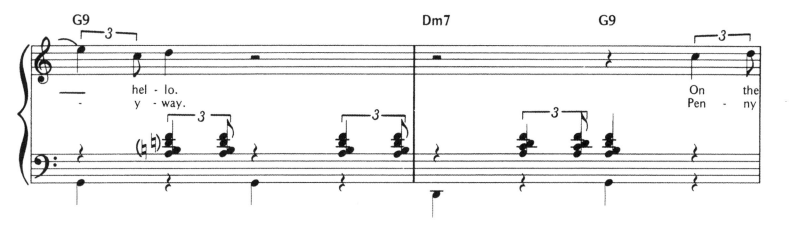

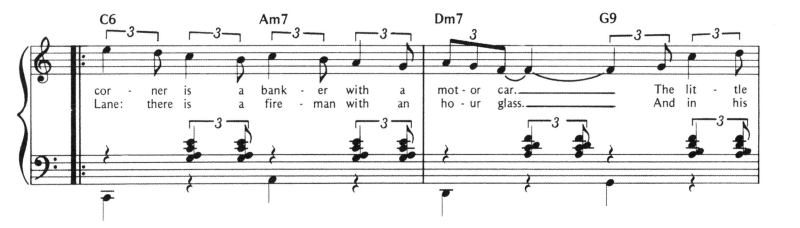

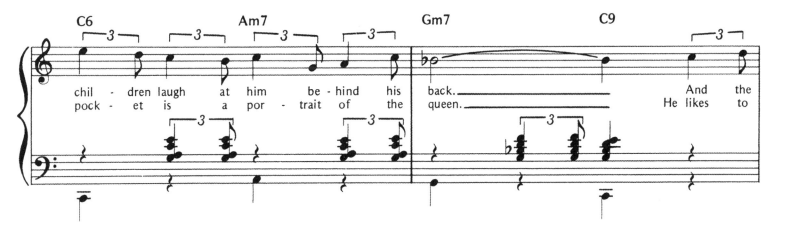

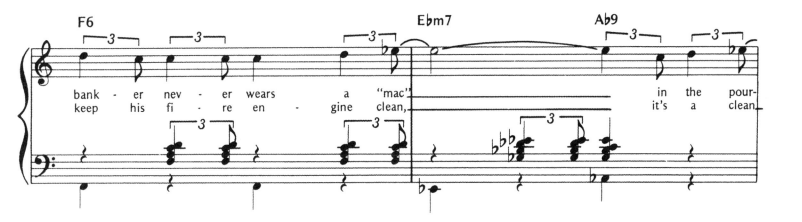

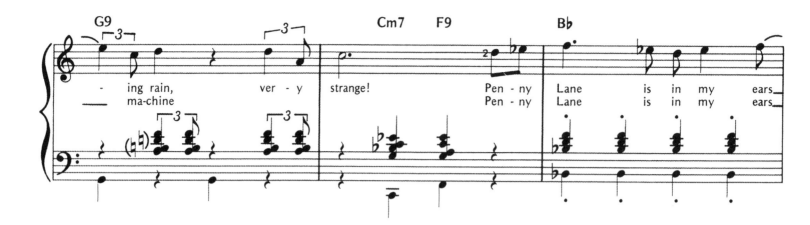

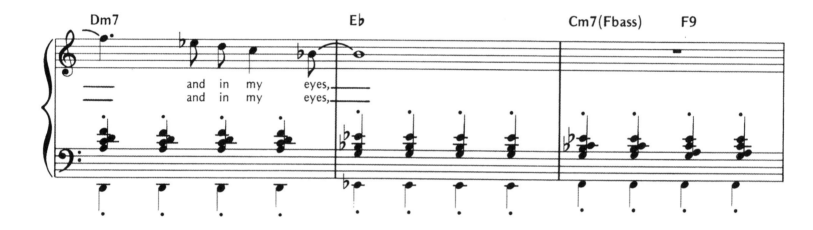

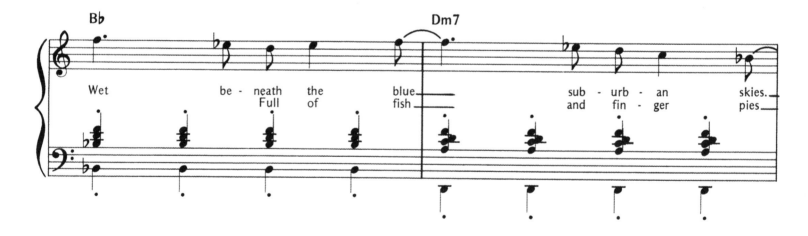

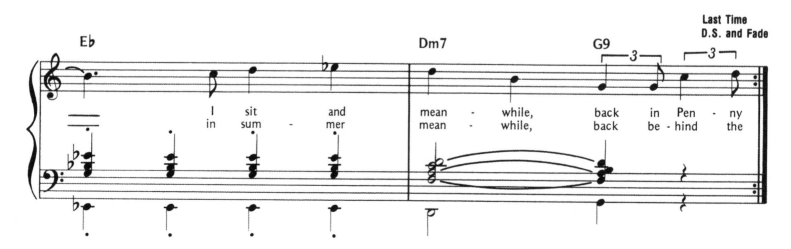

Please Please Me

Electronic Organs
Upper: Flutes (or Tibias) 16', 8', 2'
       Diapason 8'
Lower: Flutes 8', 4', String 4'
Pedal: 16'
Vib./Trem.: On, Fast

Drawbar Organs
Upper: 84 2354 757
Lower: (00) 8675 007
Pedal: 62
Vib./Trem.: On, Fast

Words and Music by John Lennon
and Paul McCartney

Moderate rock tempo

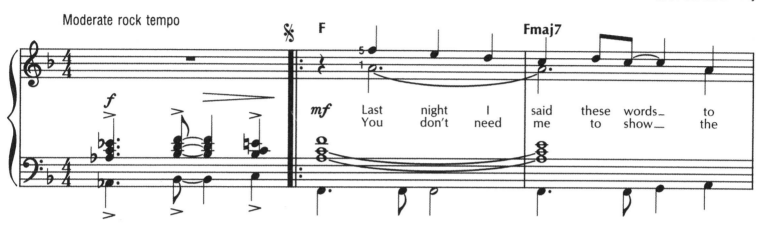

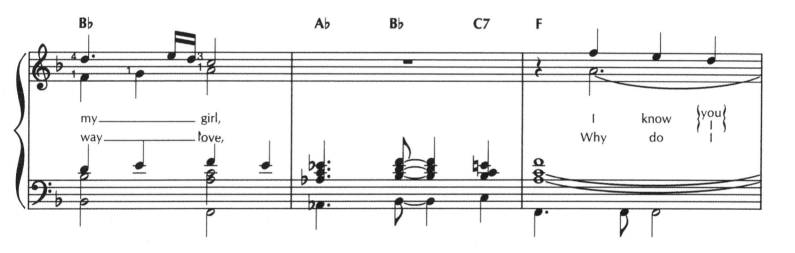

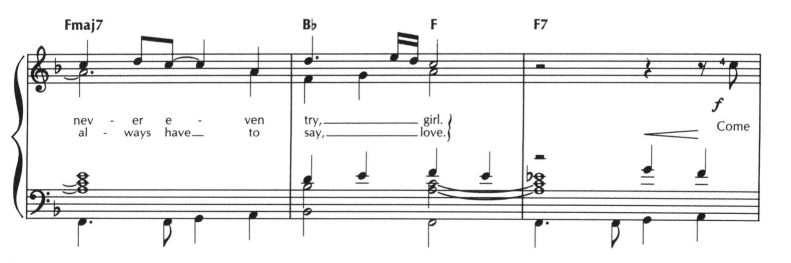

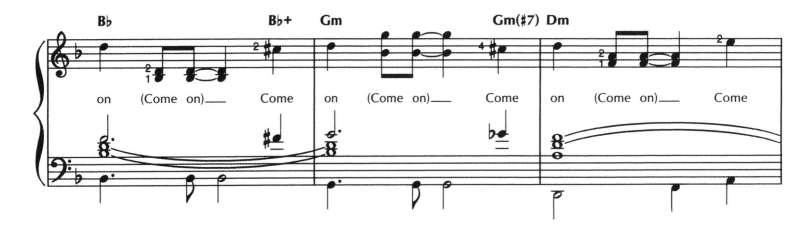

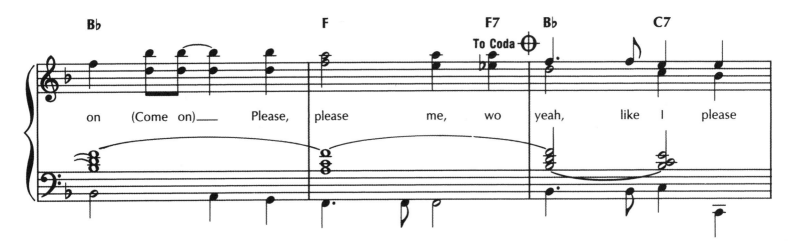

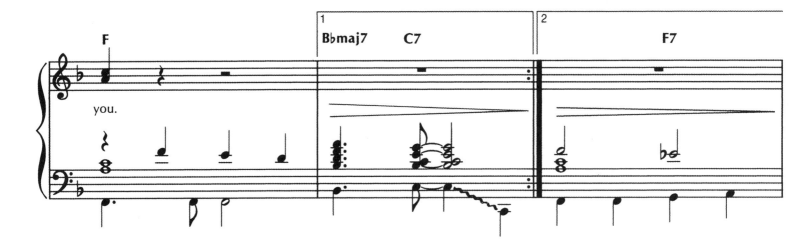

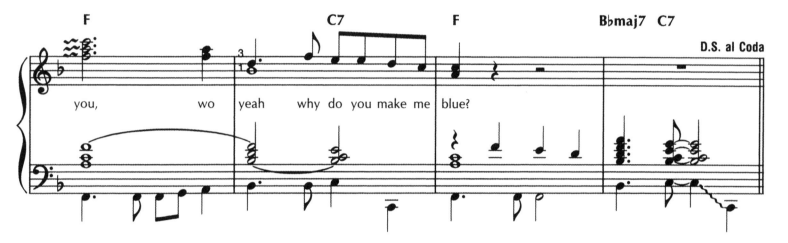

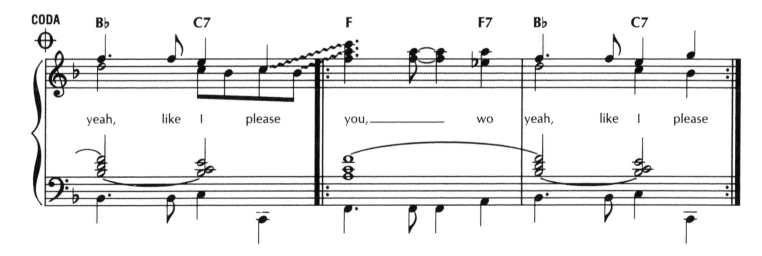

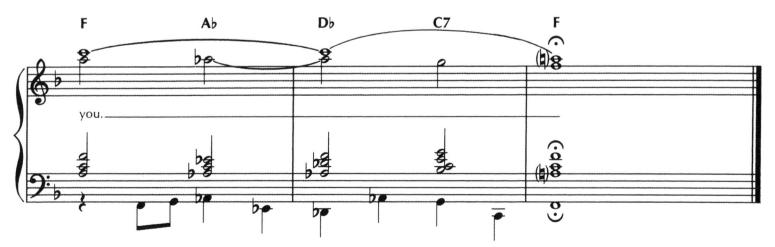

She Loves You

Electronic Organs
Upper: Preset Piano
Lower: Flutes 8', 4'
Pedal: String Bass
Vib./Trem.: On, Slow

Drawbar Organs
Upper: Preset Piano or
80 6606 000
Lower: (00) 7400 001
Pedal: String Bass
Vib./Trem.: On, Slow

Words and Music by John Lennon
and Paul McCartney

Moderate rock tempo

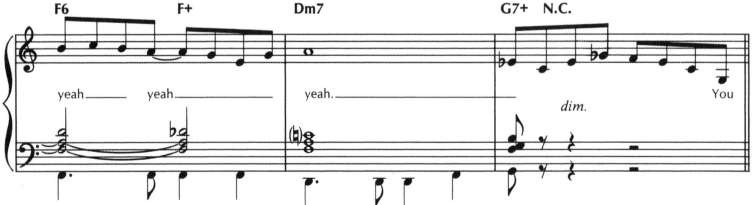

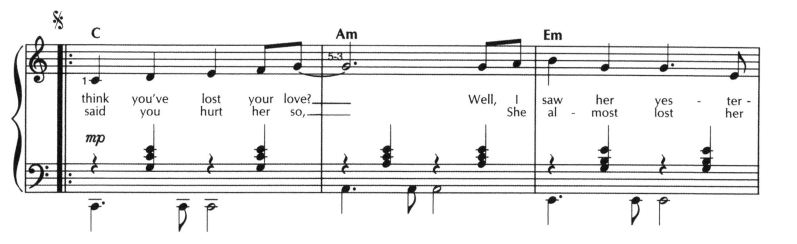

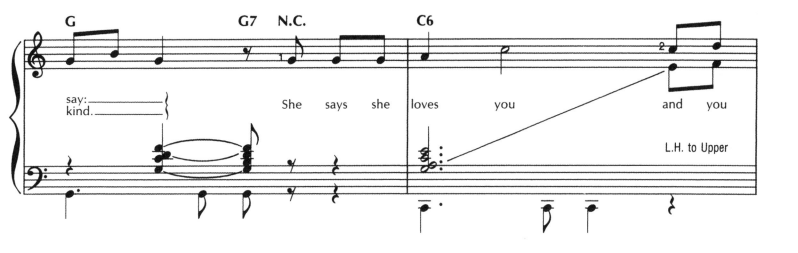

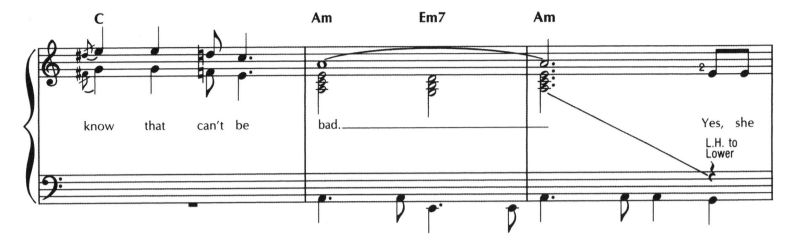

know that can't be bad._____ Yes, she

L.H. to
Lower

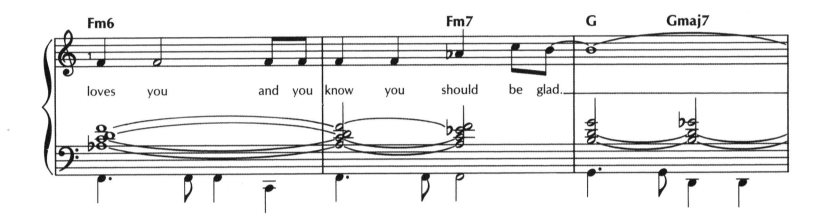

loves you and you know you should be glad.___

She___ She loves you, yeah,___

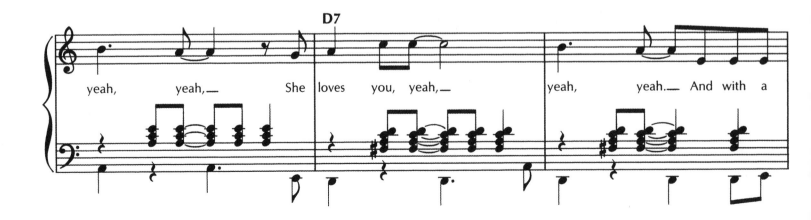

yeah, yeah,___ She loves you, yeah,___ yeah, yeah.___ And with a

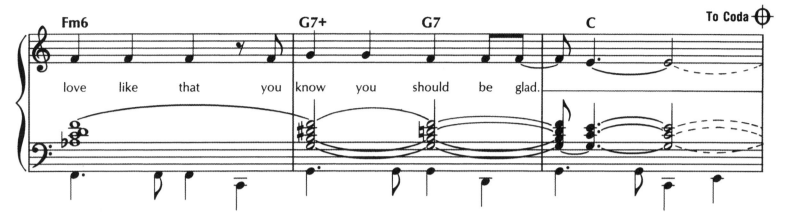

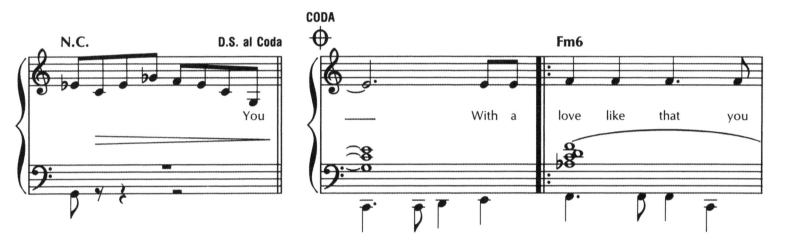

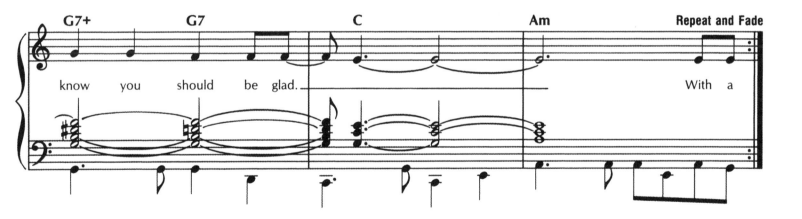

Additional Lyrics

3. (You) know it's up to you, I think it's only fair.
Pride can hurt you too, apologize to her.
Because she loves you and you know that can't be bad.
Yes, she loves you and you know you should be glad.

She loves you, yeah, yeah, yeah,
She loves you, yeah, yeah, yeah,
And with a love like that you know you should be glad.

Something

Electronic Organs
Upper: Flutes (or Tibias) 16′, 8′, 4′, 2′
Lower: Strings 8′, 4′
Pedal: String Bass
Vib./Trem.: On, Fast

Drawbar Organs
Upper: 80 6606 011
Lower: (00) 7400 000
Pedal: String Bass
Vib./Trem.: On, Fast

By George Harrison

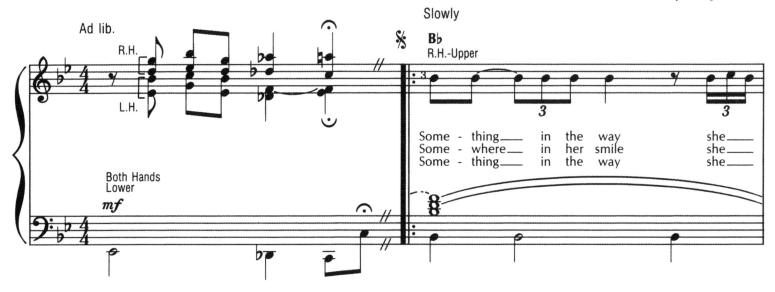

Some - thing____ in the way   she____
Some - where____ in her smile   she____
Some - thing____ in the way   she____

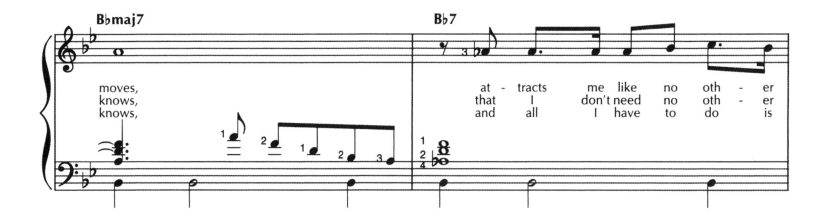

moves,   at - tracts   me like   no   oth - er
knows,   that   I   don't need   no   oth - er
knows,   and   all   I have   to   do   is

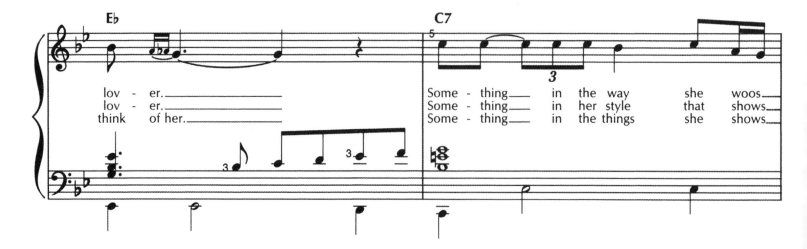

lov - er.____
lov - er.____
think of her.____

Some - thing____ in the way   she   woos,
Some - thing____ in her style   that shows,
Some - thing____ in the things   she   shows,

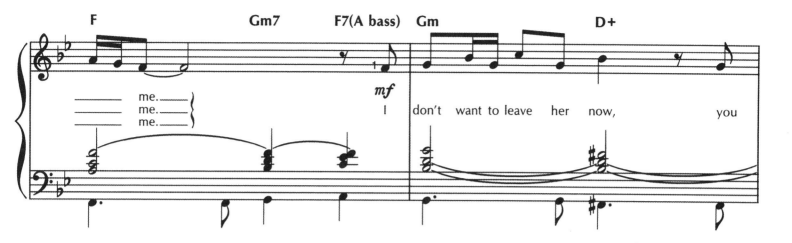

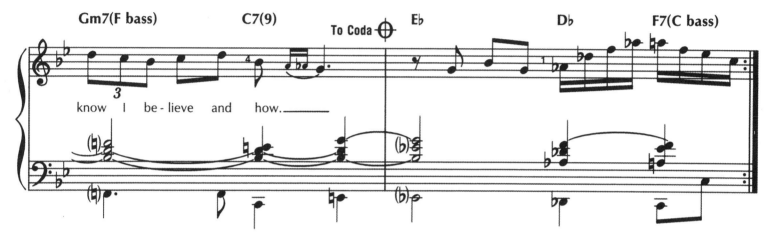

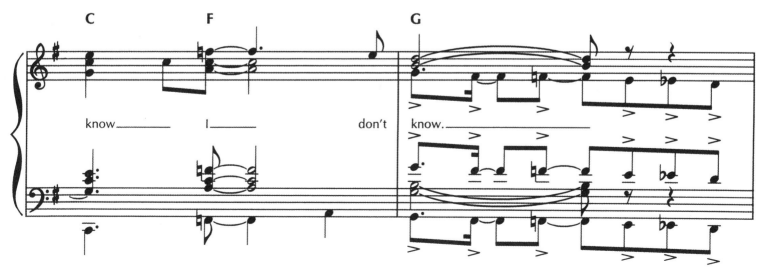

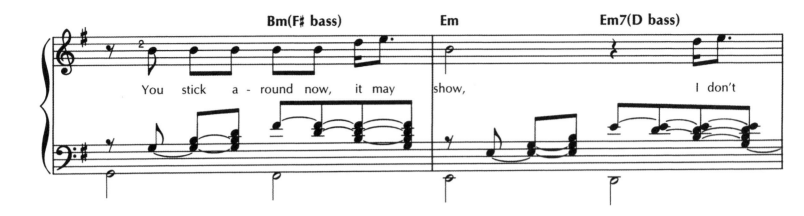

Bm(F# bass)   Em   Em7(D bass)

You stick a-round now, it may show, I don't

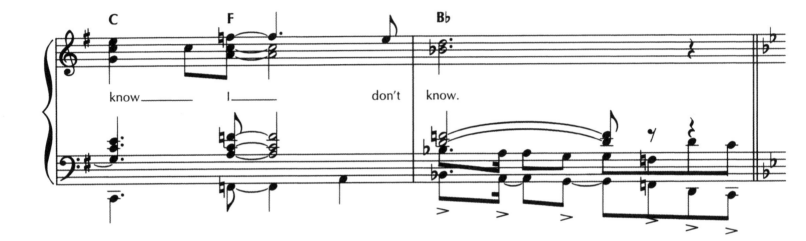

C   F   Bb

know_____ I_____ don't know.

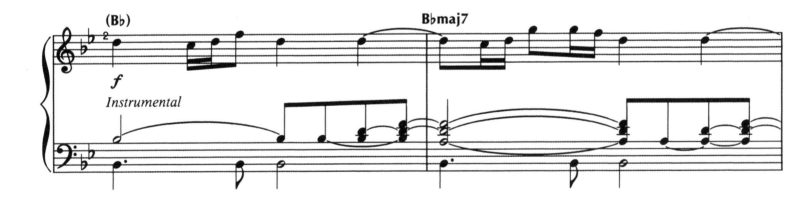

(Bb)   Bbmaj7

f

Instrumental

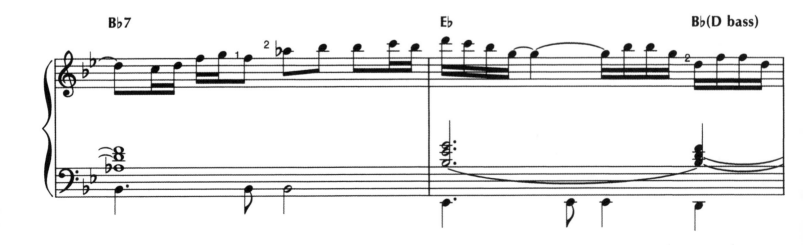

Bb7   Eb   Bb(D bass)

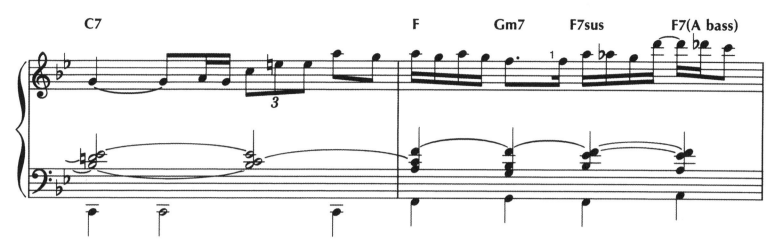

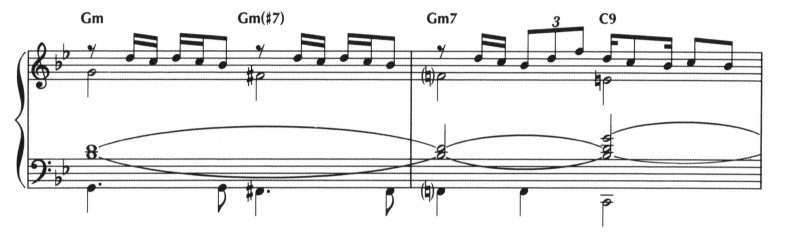

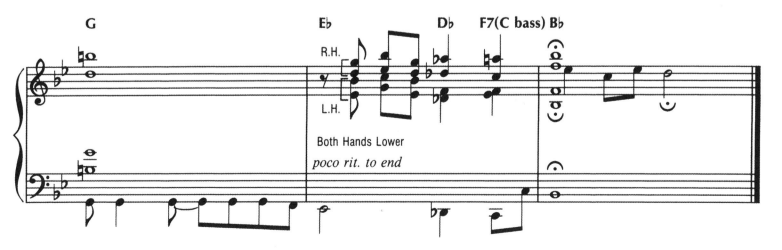

Ticket To Ride

Electronic Organs
Upper: Flutes (or Tibias) 16', 8', 4', 2'
    Clarinet
Lower: Flutes 8', 4', Reed 8'
Pedal: String Bass
Vib./Trem.: On, Fast

Drawbar Organs
Upper: 83 0313 003
Lower: (00) 6304 011
Pedal: String Bass
Vib./Trem.: On, Fast

Words and Music by John Lennon
and Paul McCartney

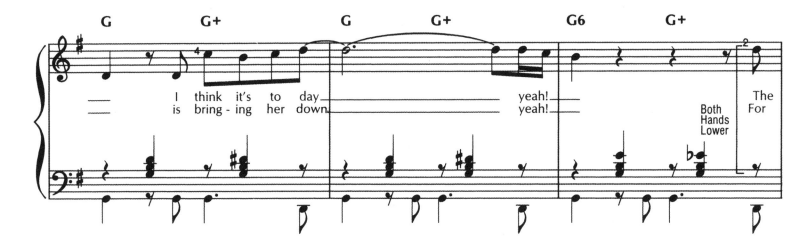

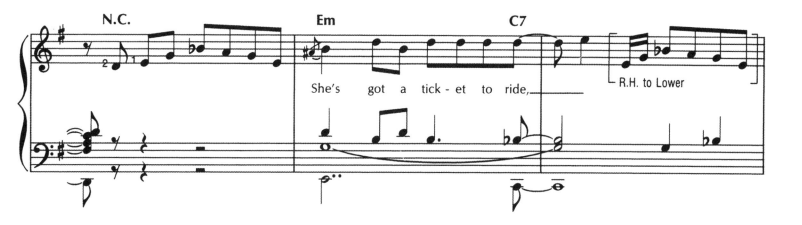

She's got a tick-et to ride,_____ R.H. to Lower

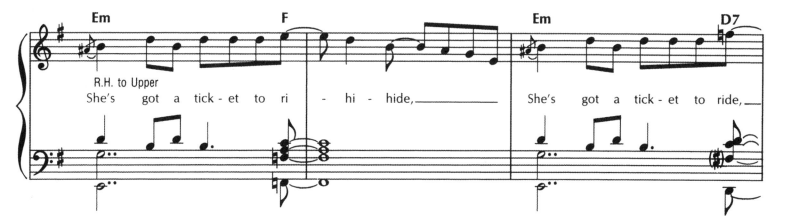

R.H. to Upper
She's got a tick-et to ri - hi - hide,_____ She's got a tick-et to ride,_____

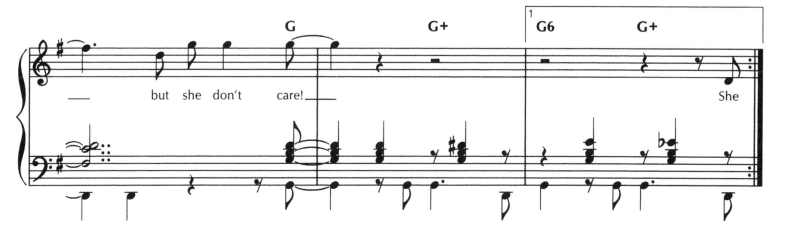

_____ but she don't care!_____ She

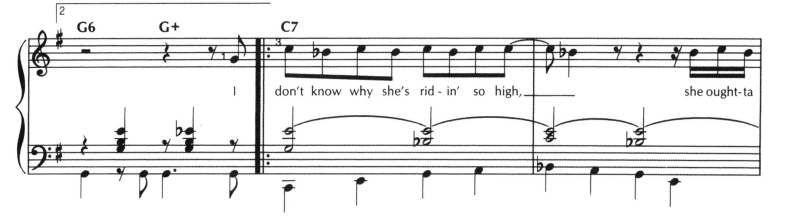

I don't know why she's rid-in' so high,_____ she ought-ta

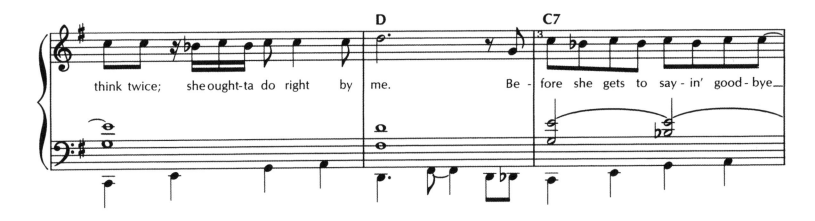

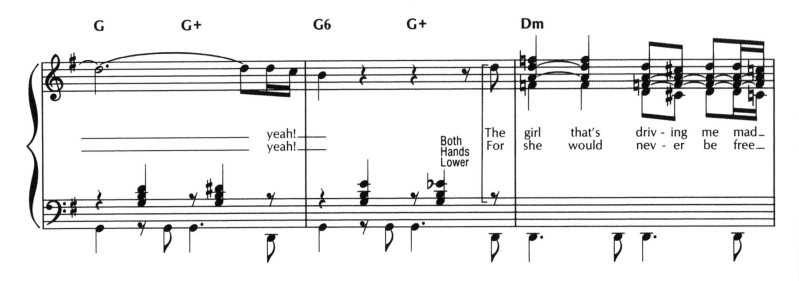

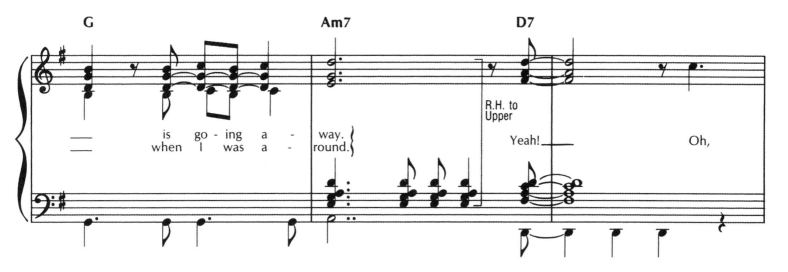

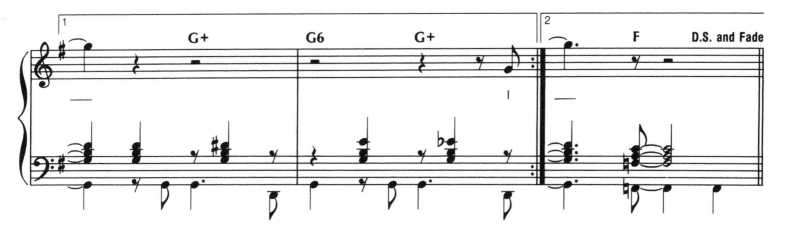

We Can Work It Out

Electronic Organs
Upper: Flutes (or Tibias) 16', 4', 2'
Lower: Flutes 8', 4'
Pedal: 8'
Vib./Trem.: On, Fast

Tonebar Organs
Upper: 60 0608 000
Lower: (00) 6500 000
Pedal: 05
Vib./Trem.: On, Fast

Words and Music by John Lennon
and Paul McCartney

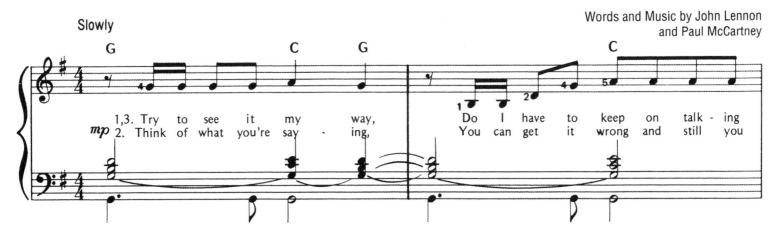

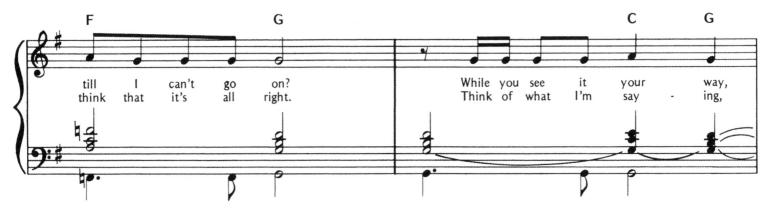

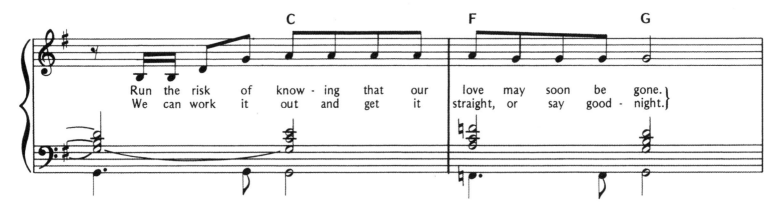

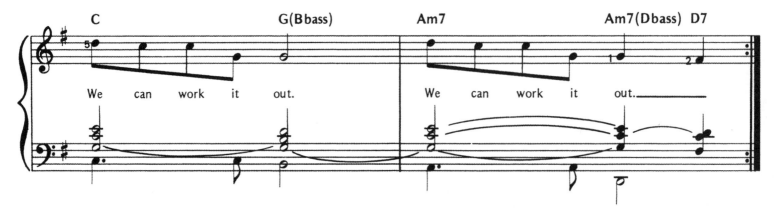

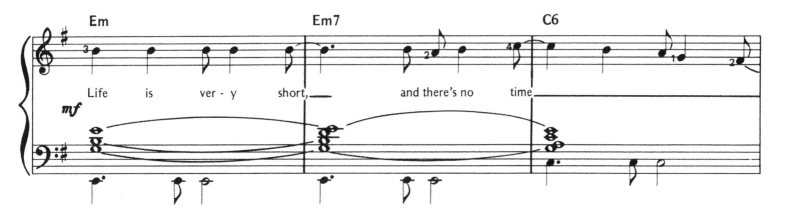

Em / Em7 / C6

Life is ver - y short,___ and there's no time___

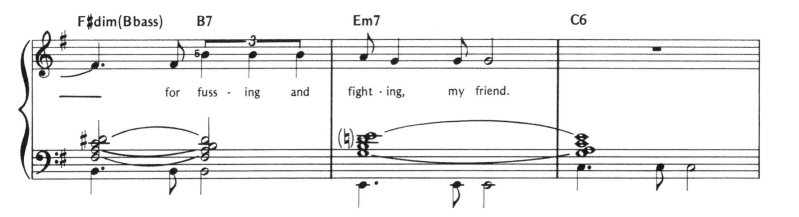

F#dim(Bbass) B7 / Em7 / C6

___ for fuss - ing and fight - ing, my friend.

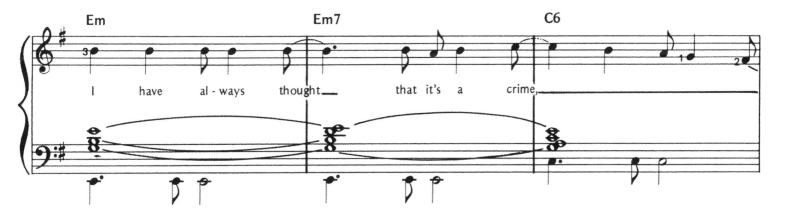

Em / Em7 / C6

I have al - ways thought___ that it's a crime,___

D.C. and Fade

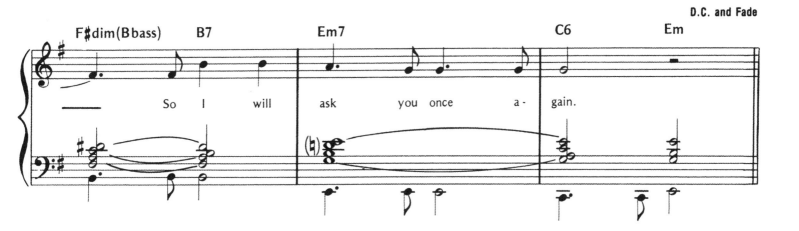

F#dim(Bbass) B7 / Em7 / C6 Em

___ So I will ask you once a - gain.

Yesterday

Electronic Organs
Upper: Flutes (or Tibias) 16′, 8′, 5⅓′,
      4′, 2′
Lower: Flutes 8′, 4′, Diapason 8′,
      Reed 8′
Pedal: 16′, 8′
Vib./Trem.: On, Fast

Tonebar Organs
Upper: 86 6606 000
Lower: (00) 7732 211
Pedal: 55
Vib./Trem.: On, Fast

Words and Music by John Lennon
and Paul McCartney

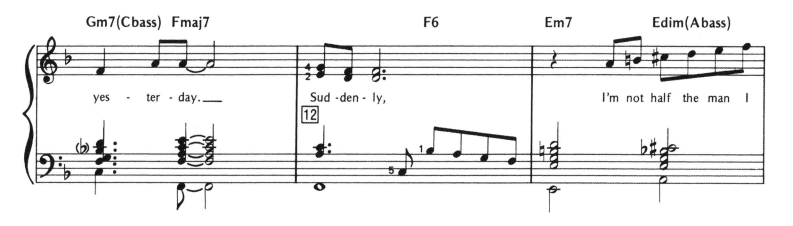

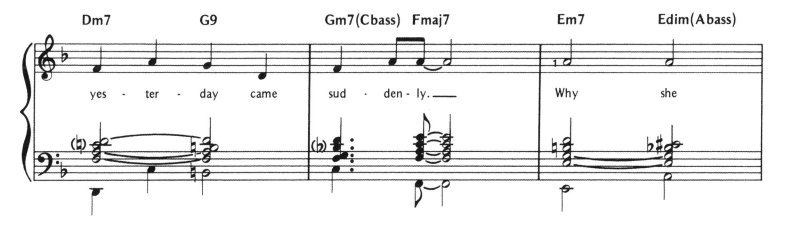

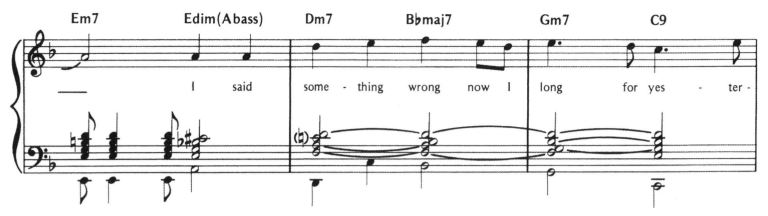

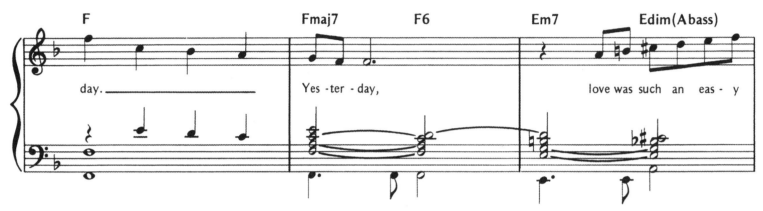

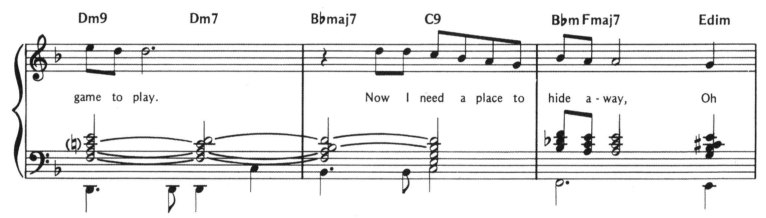

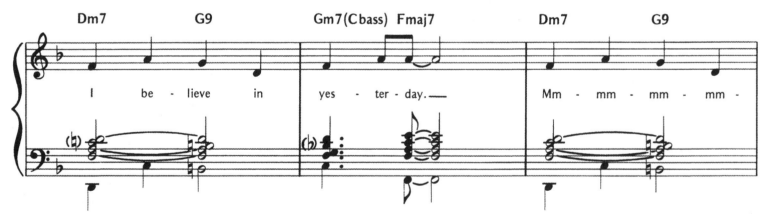